Ancient Secrets, Modern Tactics

Pure Internal Power for Fighting

By Derek Croley

Ancient Secrets, Modern Tactics

Pure Internal Power for Fighting

3

I thought about getting somebody fancy to write a forward for me. But I'm not patient enough. As I mentioned in the forward of my last book, I really got into internal martial arts because my body was a wreck. I had torn meniscus in both knees, scoliosis so I generally couldn't turn my head to the left, and nothing attaching my right shoulder on top.

I did all of this to myself sport fighting, playing football, wrestling on the school team, and generally being a very active and physical person.

With Internal Power Training, I have fixed or found pain-free workarounds for all of these things. I no longer wake up in pain and stay that way all day. So, that's nice.

So that's nice.

Anyway, with this background in fight sport, contemporary sport, and then internal art, I think I have a particular perspective on how to use internal martial arts for fighting that perhaps others do not.

I see a lot of people on YouTube trying to teach internal martial arts techniques for fighting, and a lot of them are terrible. There just isn't a real-world thought process behind their claims. Many of these people don't understand internal martial arts nor fighting anyway.

The thing is, with a proper understanding of what internal martial art is and is not, you can really get a good idea of how to actually fight with these arts. I submit that we then combine these power principles and tactics with a modern fighting art like Krav Maga.

I don't think it does us a lot of good to learn about how people fought and thought about fighting in other countries 400 years ago. It's neat, but not ultimately helpful right now.

So in this book I am going to attempt to combine authentic internal martial arts body usage and tactics with modern fighting tactics and situational awareness.

What this really means is how can we use the highest level of body awareness and understanding with our current ideas on self-defense and fighting.

Read on, and I hope you enjoy and have some things to consider in your own training!

Derek Croley

Sept 10, 2017

INTRODUCTION

AND HE JUST WALKED AWAY.

We'd been on the Sonoma Mountain training all day for the last five days. Pure internal power, kinetic testing, forms, *tui shou* (balance sparring), and application.

George Xu would come by to test each student at different times over the course of the week. He would do his best to answer questions to the absolute best of his ability and kindly but precisely point out your mistakes. He really, really wants his students to get his material, but he is uncompromising. I respect that. Makes it worth going.

Every time he touched you it was a test. An exam. A judgement of everything you'd been doing for the past year-- since last camp.

I was exhausted. We'd been working on the same sequence of basics every morning for the past week. I'd failed every test, every morning. In fact, I hadn't passed a test in three years. The last test I passed was in the parking lot, doing the Dragon Palm Baqua form. But that was three years ago.

This morning I thought I had it. I thought I'd cracked the code the night before, and I was excited to have George test me this morning. He looked at me. He touched my hand.

And he just walked away.

Fail. Not enough to comment on. I was very, very frustrated. I was angry. I wanted to go home and watch a movie. Something involving Star Wars.

It is exactly when you feel this way that it is easiest to quit. It is exactly when you feel this way that it seems smart to go home.

It is exactly when you feel like this that you absolutely, positively, without any doubt cannot stop. I see people quit all of the time, and I have no respect for them. I know where that path leads and I'm not going there. I get mad and I use that anger.

With Tai Chi and Kung Fu savant Thomas Bailor. I first met Tom in LangFang, China when he sat down next to me and said, "So Derek, what are we drinking?"

So I got back to work.

As I was practicing with a friend of mine at camp, he said something that completely clicked for me. That night in class I was once again excited to be tested by George on my newest idea. He started with the first person; she didn't pass. I could relate. The next person didn't pass. Neither did the next. The guy next to me didn't get a comment. Not good. I could relate to that as well.

It was my turn.

He tested me. Stepped back and looked at me. Then tested me again. Then stepped back and looked at me again.

Then he stepped back and said, "pass!" With as much surprise in his voice as I felt.

My hands shot up in the air in victory. I smiled uncontrollably for the next hour. It was awesome.

I hadn't passed everything forever, but I passed that.

Here's my point. It took me a while to figure this internal power thing out. It's been hard-fought. I've been at it for 35 years. I get more things wrong than I get right, but I don't stop. Ever.

I WANT THE SECRETS.

When I was a kid I was inspired by the hero's journey. I was inspired by seeking out truth and hard-fought knowledge. I was inspired to do what others would not, so I could learn what others weren't willing to put forth the effort to. And I have. I could've taken many different paths in life, but I chose this one. After 35 years of training I'm still not finished. There is no end to knowledge.

I'm going to try to explain these secrets to you in as plain English as I can.

And there are secrets. Some say there are no secrets; they either don't know any or don't want to tell them to you. None of the secrets to martial arts are magic, and none of them are easy.

Some of the things that I wrote in the last book I will contradict in this one. At the time I am writing this five years have gone by and I have not been complacent. There will be no going back to revise the last volume as what I wrote at the time was the truth to the best of my knowledge at the time, and it is certainly still valid. I've just learned more.

When I lived in Jilin City in Northeastern China, I was fortunate enough to get to train with *Liu Chan Shan*, pictured above. He taught me the secret single-step art of *Yuan Gong Chan Chuan*. Interestingly, the secrets of this secret art are not all that secret, but it is certainly a unique interpretation of the things I will outline in this book.

I won't go into what the "secret techniques" are, at least not for now, but I merely want to point out that, yes, there are secret arts; there are things that are not common knowledge.

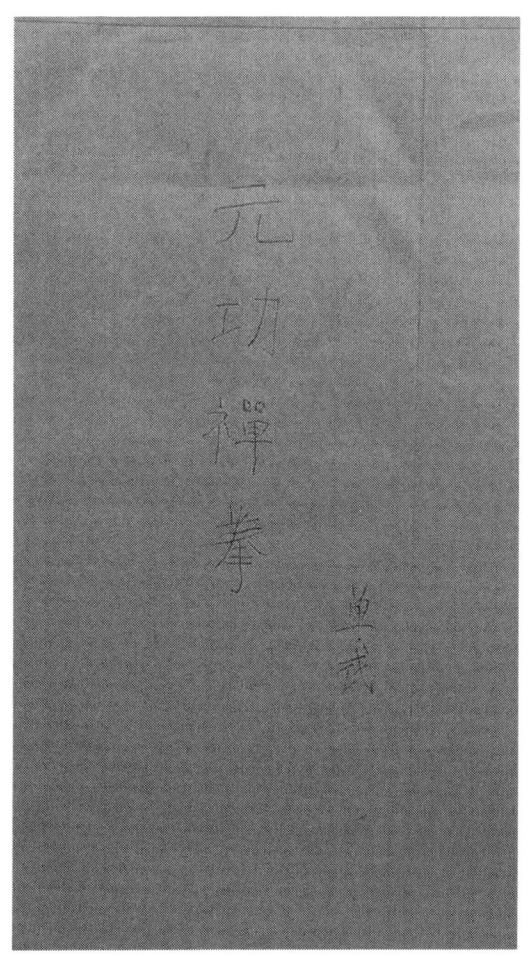

This is the cover of the book Shifu Liu Chan Shan wrote for me on the secret art of Yuan Gong Chan Chuan. He gave it to me in 1999 as a practice guide, by my lack of ability to read Chinese has hindered that greatly.

JUST KEEP TRAINING

I continue to train with George Xu in Chinese internal martial arts and have made great strides. Every year I go to his week-long training camp at the Sonoma Zen Center in California. I then work on his lessons from camp for a whole year. The material is technical enough that it just takes me that long to process what he is teaching.

Remember, this isn't a race. It is a path. Your goal is to just keep putting one foot in front of the other, and over the course of your life you will become extraordinary. Achieving a high level at anything is not about one big moment, one big score. It is about doing the little things with greater and greater refinement for a long period of time. It is about finding the coaches and teacher who can help you and point out your mistakes.

For example, as I write this book I need someone to proofread it as I simply cannot see my mistakes. The same is true for all endeavors that you are serious about. Learn to take constructive criticism. Learn to revel in it.

Also, I have continued to train in Krav Maga under Ernie Kirk, even traveling with him to train at the Wingate Institute in Israel. This is the birthplace of Krav Maga, and I learned a great deal there.

I really enjoy training with Ernie. The way he moves and thinks about things is very different from me, and I have learned a lot from this. He is an excellent example of high-level thought and refinement-- even though I seriously doubt if he considers himself refined. But he is. He travels the world to train with the best people he can find in Krav Maga. His quest for knowledge is inspiring to me.

And finally, I have focused a lot on training under Bill "Superfoot" Wallace in kickboxing. He is noted for his kicking, and his talents do lie there, but his genius lies in his understanding of tactics. Bill has been a major name in the martial arts industry since before there was a martial arts industry. Right along with Chuck Norris, he is an icon and a legend for people my age. He was the first middle-weight kickboxing champion, retiring undefeated, and after that I think he's been in every issue of Black Belt magazine ever. He also has traveled the world for decades teaching and learning about martial arts.

These three men are very different, but have some things in common. I have learned a lot from all of them, and I will continue to train. As should you.

All three of these men offer some incredible insights into body dynamics, martial techniques, and of course tactics. I highly recommend that you train with any of them whenever possible.

Some people even come to train with me. Weird.

Different people train in the martial arts for different reasons. For me it was and still is a vision quest. I have always been interested in the pursuit of personal growth and personal understanding. Looking to find myself through experience, I moved to China for about a year when I was 24. This came to be a huge part of who and what I am, how I define myself.

One of the things that Bill Wallace talked about the last time I saw him was a little bit of his life story-- which is pretty interesting. He spoke of how there really were three different choices in his life that took him in the direction he went. The story of what those choices were is his to tell, but the point is that there are often just a few, often seemingly unimportant at the time, choices that we all make that take us in specific directions that become life-altering. I suspect living in China was one of mine.

I know many people who went into sport martial arts and tournaments for their vision quest. I know others who joined the military. I know many who lacked that certain something to ever take their journey. It's never too late.

For me, I did numerous tournaments in fighting and forms and didn't find it gratifying. No disrespect to those who do. I came of age after kickboxing was a thing and before MMA was a twinkle in Dana White's eye. So it was mostly point karate and forms.

Then I did stupid things like getting into fights as a young man just for the fun of it. I strongly recommend that you not do the same, but I was looking for myself. Some of the places I looked were the wrong places.

Whatever your personal journey is, whatever your vision quest needs to be, take it.

Another idea that is prevalent is the notion that traditional training methods do not work in the real world of martial arts. This is unfortunately true, but also not. It's the training method, not the art.

What I mean by this is that just doing forms over and over again will not train you to fight, but it will train you to get really good at movement. To get good at fighting all you have to do is fight. Do stress drills. Spar. The art isn't the problem, it the training method.

I tend to go back to "The Seven Habits of Highly Effective People," by Covey as a go-to for how to design your training method. Think about what you want to accomplish and then work on how to get there.

FOCUSES OF TRAINING

There are three areas of martial training:

1. Martial Art
2. Martial Sport
3. Martial real-world conflict

Martial Art is forms, basics, and other forms of training that are about learning a physical art. This includes cultural dance, or forms, and is great for people who want to get in better shape, learn something cool, and study a physical art.

By the way, a friend of mine, Scott Phillips, wrote a very interesting book on forms called "Possible Origins: A Cultural History of Chinese Martial Arts, Theater and Religion." This book is pretty specific to Chen Style Tai Chi, but that doesn't really matter. He presents a compelling argument regarding fighting, religion, dance, and history being an important part of culture and how these elements would have been blended into cultural dance (i.e. forms, katas, etc).

This book is genius.

Master Ken is also a genius. Check out his Youtube show; he gets it. As a side note, my kid looked at this picture and said, "Getting a belly, Dad?" I don't think so, but this sure is an unflattering picture of me isn't it. Why did I even put this in my own book?

I also really enjoyed a book recommended my by good friend, World Champion kickboxer Kevin Hudson. To be fair, Kevin has written his own book about his personal story that is pretty awesome called "You Can Hit the Mark," and you should absolutely read it, but right now I'm talking about "Shotokan's Secret: The Hidden Truth Behind Karate's Fighting Origins," by Bruce Clayton.

I don't even do Shotokan, but I think this is an important book.

Both of these books talk about the reason for practicing martial art as physical art, as well as other important cultural reasons. Physical art and personal expression through art is nothing to sneeze at and should never be overlooked. Also, traditional martial arts teach us a great deal about techniques, body awareness, and fights tactics with case study examples, and even physical fitness. All good martial artists I know have at some time in their education gotten at least a Black Belt level in something. Some arts don't do belts, but they still have some rite of passage, some level of attainment that is similar. This is what I am talking about.

Next is martial sport. Kickboxing, tournament forms, point fighting, and weapons, MMA, submission grappling, etc, are all awesome in their own right. All are sport and should be treated as such. The very existence of rules means that none of these are self-defense, yet it is irrefutable that the lessons learned from participating in any of these sports are highly valuable in a self-defense situation.

Last is martial real-world conflict. With this I'm thinking of real-world fighting. For civilians this is self-defense, but could also include police and military fighting tactics. Each is different. I am writing this book with civilian tactics and techniques in mind.

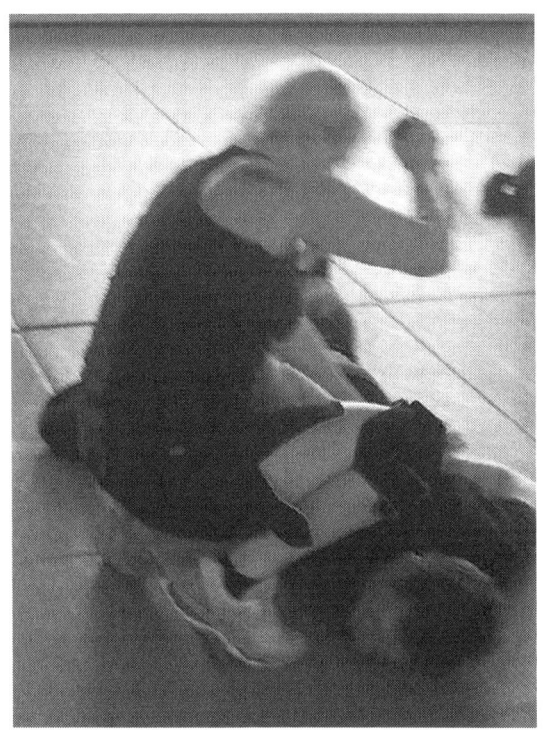

This was taken in Israel at the Wingate Institute. We were practicing knife disarms. I'm not sure if that knife is going towards me or away from me.

Remember, there is a difference between self-defense and violence. **Violence is actively trying to hurt somebody else, while self-defense is actively trying to not get hurt.** All martial art, from my perspective, should always be self-defense.

Take that! And that and that and that!!!

This type of training involves safe but realistic stress drills designed to make you face the situations and physiological reactions you might experience in a real attack. Some of these are pretty fun, and some are pretty difficult. What's interesting about stress drills is that they tend to very specifically point out the difference between what your body knows and what your mind knows. What I mean by this is that in stress drills you will do things that you know you shouldn't do in self-defense situations. This is good because you learn how you respond to situations and stress. This gives you a very good idea of how you should train for real situations, and this will be specific to you and how your mind and body respond to stress.

Here's the thing: you get good at what you train for. It doesn't matter what "style" you do. What matters is how you train. I submit that you should do all three. You should know something about art, you should learn the lessons of sport, and you should learn the tactics of fighting for real.

Art doesn't have to follow reality, sport has rules that protect and limit you, and real bad guys don't follow any particular rules, but whatever they do is real and designed to hurt you. So, train for all three. Which one should you focus on the most? That's up to you and your interests.

I only suggest that whatever you do, understand what you are doing. If you only do traditional forms then of course you can't fight for real. If you only do stress drills for self-defense purposes then of course you don't understand the nuances of forms. I suggest that you need to know something of all three, even though you will probably specialize in one aspect of martial training.

Kevin Hudson punching one of my Instructors. Robert doesn't like it when I take pictures of his face because he's so pretty.

Always remember that your goal is personal growth and improvement. Any other reason for training is not good enough.

There are two big mistakes people make as they try to pursue information about martial arts. First, people want to mystify Internal Power, Chi, and so on. Don't do this. As soon as you do that, you will create your own glass ceiling.

One time I had a guy who was a black belt at a competing school call me to inquire about taking lessons with me. Based upon our conversation, I gleaned that he mostly wanted to hear himself talk and didn't really want to train, so I kind of zoned out there a lot over the course of the conversation. Anyway, this black belt fellow loved to hear himself talk, and when I told him that we did internal martial arts his pontification began with, "well, that is always the goal isn't it?" And then he went on about something or another. He was completely in la la land.

Nonsense. You get what you train for. If you are training in an external martial art you will not achieve internal anything. You get the result from the work that you do. Training is funny that way.

Here's the thing. If you mystify your goals you make them unattainable and unreachable. Therefore, you will not be able to train in the right direction. Don't do this to yourself.

Remember, right thought combined with right action equals the right result.

The second big mistake people make is to not be clear on which aspect of training they are trying to train. What is internal and what is not? What is chi and what is physical? What is the difference between your imagination and chi and spirit? It can be very confusing. Let's lay this out.

JING, CHI, AND SHEN.

First off, we need to establish what internal power is and isn't. There are three main aspects to body quality training. It is important to be clear about what is what. These three things are *Jing, Chi,* and *Shen.*

It took me a long time to become clear on what is what, so please do take this part seriously. It will make your life so much easier.

Shockingly, this isn't magic. It all boils down to

F=MA. Force=Mass x Acceleration

Yeah, sorry. Math.

It works best if you think of *jing* as force, *chi* as kinetic energy, and *shen* as your ability to focus on your opponent or what you are doing (potential energy).

Hey, before we get started on these three things, I want to mention a little bit about Structure since it's talked about so much.

STRUCTURE AND ROOTING

For large portions of my martial arts career, the thing to do has been to stand in deep stances for long periods of time, holding one or more of your four limbs out in the air for as long as possible. For years this was taught as a great way to get strong enough to do martial arts.

.

I even had one teacher who would walk by and hit you with his hand or a stick to toughen you up. "You need to build strong structure and get more rooted," they said. Get more rooted. Get more rooted. Get more rooted.

Nah. You need to learn to move.

Look at how rooted James Brown was as he moved all over the stage. Yeah, he wasn't. But his balance was great, his hips were relaxed, and his head wasn't past his feet.

You do need to learn how to align your skeleton, but we need to get past this as soon as possible. We don't want to focus too much on your skeletal structure, rather we want to focus on movement.

You need to be balanced. You need to be relaxed. And you need to be able to move.

The basic rule of thumb regarding structure is to stand in a way that you feel balanced but can move in any direction. This boils down to three things:

1. **Relax your hip extenders.**
2. **Have your weight a bit more on the balls of your feet.**
3. **Don't let your head get outside of your feet.**

Relaxing your hip extender is important as it allows you to have hip mobility and therefore move.

Having your weight a bit more on the balls of your feet enables you to move.

If your head goes to any given direction, the rest of you will follow, so don't let your head get past your feet.

In class I sometimes half joke that if your feet aren't under your head, somebody else's foot will be under your head. And it'll hurt when you wake up.

Story of my life. Getting bounced off the ground by George. But look at the position he has on me. Even though this was just a cooperative demonstration, he still has great stability.

See how everything in his body attaches to his core and then to the ground? Even as he holds my leg up it is supported by the earth.

STRUCTURE TESTING.

As I said a moment ago, we don't want to spend forever on structure; we want to get it basically right and then move on.

First, have somebody push straight down on your shoulders. If your hips are too far forward, you will feel pressure in your lower back, belly, and thighs. If you are straight you will feel like you are being pushed on, but there will be no feeling of weakness anywhere.

Second, have somebody push on your forehead. If your spine is transferring the power from their push downward, all is good. If you feel pressure in your neck or lower back, you need to adjust your spine and head so the force from their push goes downward; the neck should be relaxed for this exercise.

And that's pretty much it. You can have people push on you in other places, chest, belly, shoulder, back, and so on- but you're just testing the same thing over and over again. Don't go too crazy with it.

We really need to learn how to move, not how to stand. This is the part that gives most people problems. They can do great if they just have to relax and stand there, but as soon as they have to move, everything goes wrong.

This is because standing still also trains the muscles incorrectly. It takes different things in your body to move than to stand still in a posture. We need to train the things that facilitate movement.

For example, your triceps extend your arm and your serratus holds your arm up during movement. However, holding your arm up with no movement uses the deltoid and bicep. The exact opposite muscles we need to be using to create the movement we want.

If you go to a martial art school where they make you stand in any given posture for long periods of time, you should go home.

Become a student of movement. Become a student of change. I know this statement is one that no traditional martial artist will agree with. I'm sure something like "you should begin with structure and then...." Is going through some of my readers heads.

Nonsense. I thought that way for a while as well, but how well does a flag pole fight?

Study movement and how to use your body during movement. Do not waste your time standing still in a horse stance punching the air. Do not waste your time standing in a meditative state for hours on end.

Spend your time on movement. Study footwork in fighting. Study how to use an effective lead step.

Study how to move your head. Study how to chamber your knee while kicking a bag. Study how to run. Study how to sidestep.

If you are of a more philosophical bent, go outside and study how the world moves. Study how people grow and change. Study how the seasons change.

Nothing is ever still. Nothing. Don't waste your time practicing being still. Practice paying attention to movement.

Some people wish to achieve stillness in their minds, but there is no such thing as stillness. There is balance, there is harmony, but there is not stillness. Find harmony with your motion. Find balance with your environment. This is achieved through understanding movement.

JING

Jing is force. For a long time I didn't have this quite right. I thought *jing* was just using your physical body. This was mostly because people would use the word *jing* as a synonym for 'body' as far as I could tell, so I kind of inferred that was what it meant. Not quite. Force is the point where there is a transfer of energy. Of course, the way you use your body is very important to how much force you can generate. The greater percentage of your mass you can use, the better, and the more you can accelerate it, the better.

This is pretty interesting if you think about it. If we look at the martial art application of these ideas, the big goal is always to hit or lock the other person. The big idea is always to generate force. There are a few ways this can play out if you are hitting somebody.

First, you are successful in hitting a vital target and something bad happens to the bad guy. Second, they block it. Third, they evade your attack altogether.

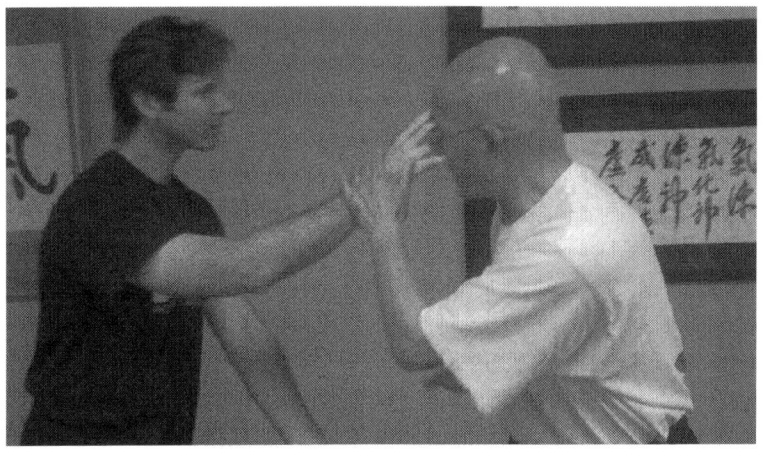

I know I'm stating the obvious here, but stick with me.

Here is where the internal part comes into play. What if you could layer your technique, balance, point of leverage, and power base? With internal power, the initial point of contact, the initial location of force, doesn't have to be the end point of your kinetic energy.

This means that just because somebody blocks your punch you can still continue the technique. This will make sense as we go over more of this concept.

Let's look at more stuff to get a better grip on this.

CHI

Chi is the energy created by movement. *Chi* by definition is change. The change in a given system. This means that *chi* is kinetic energy. All living things have chi because all living things move and change. Our bodies move and change. The seasons move and change. Relationships move and change. You get the idea-- all things have *chi*.

Talking about our bodies, *chi* as it pertains to
medicine is different than *chi* as it pertains to
movement. For our purposes of Martial Art, don't
worry too much about vessels and meridians and other
medical things that you will read about a lot. It does
come in a little handy when thinking about vital
targets to hit on the bad guy, but even then don't make

it too complicated. Hit bad guys where you do not want to be hit. That's pretty much it.

Here's why. Vital point hitting is useful, but only on a gross level. What I mean is hitting people in the eyes, nose, neck, solar plexus, ribs, groin, knee….hit the basics. Getting too much more complicated is impractical in fighting.

Pressure points are real, but vital target hitting like that is really only useful for medical purposes. Otherwise fights are too fast, with too much variability, and too much movement. You can't hit complicated special points in a specific sequence at a specific depth from a specific angle reliably in a fight.

So, don't worry about pressure-point fighting. It's impractical.

Human body meridians

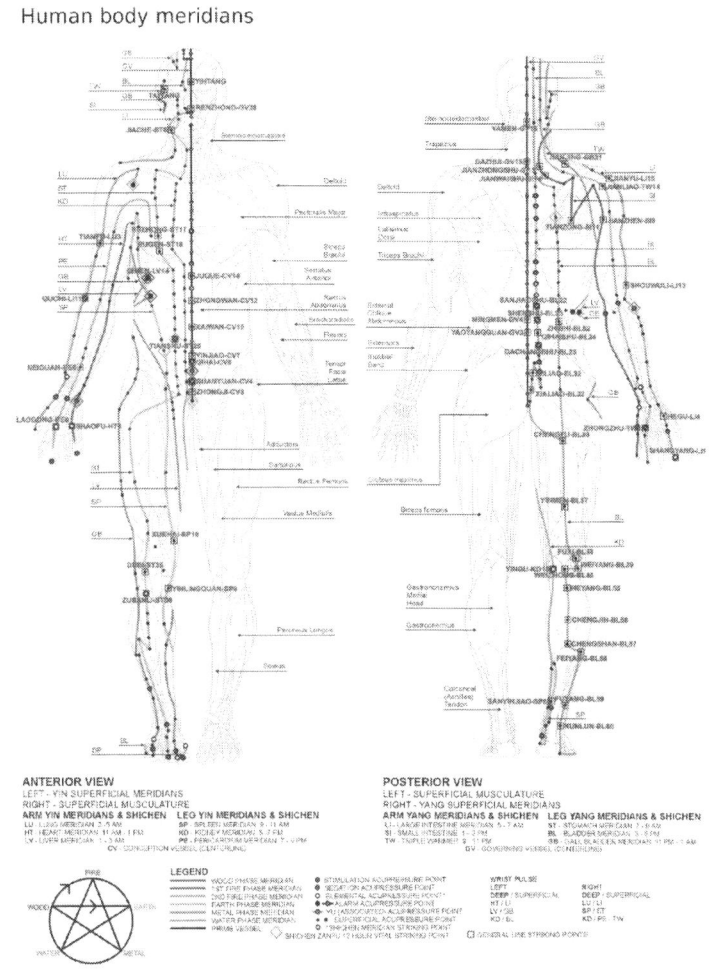

Thank you Wikipedia for this picture.

For our purposes, *chi* is in reference to the energy you generate by moving your body. The aforementioned acceleration (Force=Mass x *Acceleration*) is of course *chi*.

It is important to be able to distinguish where you are generating your *chi*, or energy, from.

Wei Chi is external chi, and ***Nei Chi*** is internal *chi*. *Wei chi* is generated by the use of external movement. This is of course important. To throw a punch you must learn how to shift your weight, rotate your hips, use your footwork, etc. *Nei chi* is energy generated by the internal muscles such as the psoas, diaphragm, and gluteus maximus.

All good martial artists end up having both internal and external *chi*. This is good, but ultimately, we want to have only internal as it is difficult to defend against and we are only using very strong parts of your body. We want to be able to completely relax the muscles that are not useful to your movement and only use the ones that are helpful to what you are doing.

To be clear, *chi* is the energy created by the use of your body. It can be thought of as the energy that you are generating.

The interesting thing about *chi* is that it becomes a thing in and of itself that you can manage and manipulate with your mind. At first you think about what you are doing with your body, and it is important to build your knowledge of how to use your body correctly, then build the skill sets to actually do it. Once you can do that, then change your focus from your muscles and so on to your *chi*. Working with the energy created by your body turns into thinking and perceiving yourself as just being a "*chi* body." Then you just think about moving *chi* around.

SHEN

Shen is 'spirit.' For our purposes, let's consider this the combination of mind, intention, focus, and will.

Again, this can be divided up as *Nei Shen* (Internal Spirit), and *Wei Shen* (external spirit). Only in this case, internal means that you are focused on yourself and external means that you are focused on what is around you.

This is the calligraphy from the first George Xu Camp I attended, I think, in 2006. Every camp he gives the participants a shirt with the theme of the camp written in Chinese Calligraphy. This, of course, says 'Spirit.'

Obviously, we would prefer to get to the point that your body knows what to do and you no longer need to pay attention to it; you can pay attention to your opponent and environment.

What we really want to do in all cases is make the internal and external reverse. We want the Yin to become Yang and the Yang to become Yin.

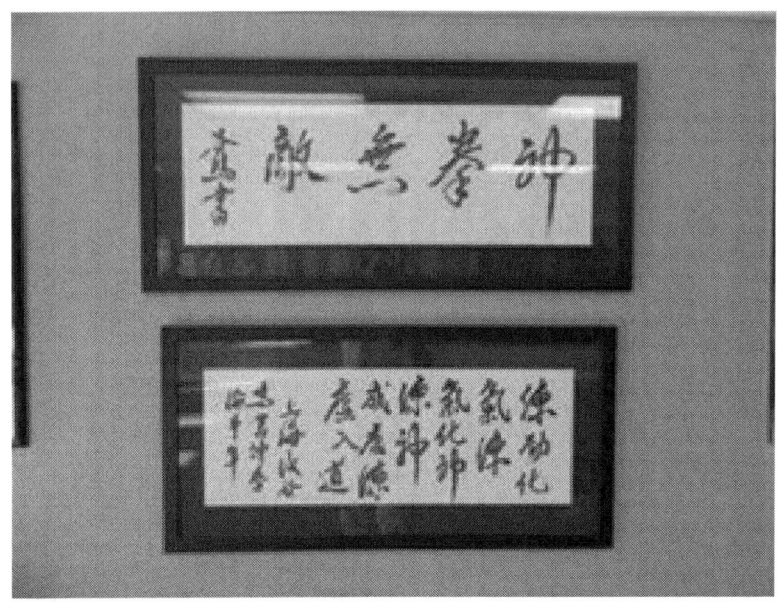

This is some custom calligraphy that George wrote for me several years ago. For years I had it on the wall of my classroom. Recently I moved them to my office as the frames were getting some damage. The top one says, "Spiritual Fist Undefeatable Secrets," while the bottom one is a discussion on moving from Jing, to Chi, to Shen, to Taiji, and then to Wuji.

George Xu, my teacher and the dude that pretty much all of these internal power ideas came from, explains this as looking for the negative space. To figure this out he had me looking at impressionistic art. He is a

Van Gogh fan while I personally prefer Monet. Anyway, he would say to learn to play with what is real and what is not real. In your art be like the impressionists. What you are doing is not totally realism, and yet it is not totally abstract. It is both and neither.

I figured this out looking at Water Lilies.

Claude Monet was the bomb, yo. Most importantly though, look at how the negative space creates the positive space.

He was playing the space, not the subject. Impressionism is exactly what martial art should be.

Real but not real, abstract but not abstract.

That Van Gogh guy was pretty awesome as well. I personally favor Monet, but this guy is also amazing.

Look at how he's used texture to create. Every individual stroke creates a part of the whole.

Again, just like Monet, Van Gogh was playing the negative space to create the positive space. He just did it differently.

Playing the negative space. Did you ever watch Fred Astaire, Michael Jackson, or James Brown (my favorite) dance? They played the space around the dance.

From Wikipedia

Go onto YouTube and watch some old videos of Fred Astaire and Ginger Rogers tap dancing. She is an absolute master, but he is a master of emptiness. Just wow. If you watch, he is suspended from a point above his head as he dances, allowing him to be completely free. He is not even in his body as he moves, he's just empty. Ginger is amazing as well, but her focus is on herself as she dances, perhaps it's the heels she joked about.

I'm not a super big Rolling Stones fan, but Mick Jagger does this with his voice. It's not just being loud or even technically proficient.

Look up Kate Smith singing "God Bless America." A perfect example of this. Her voice is the technique, and it's amazing. But then there is a certain something underneath the voice, an internal power. But then after that you notice that her mind and spirit are behind the audience. An amazing display of the principles in this book.

From Wikipedia

How I like to begin the discussion of interpretation of this idea is with the idea of reversing everything. Figure out a concept, any concept, and then try to figure out the equal but opposite aspect of it.

Most people use their bodies with what we call ox power, using only external muscles. Reverse that with the use of bone, ligament, and tendon. We call this going from bad body quality to good body quality.

But then can you go from the good body quality, or external power, to internal power? Most trained fighters use internal power and external power together. Separate them, learn to be pure internal.

If you can go from external physical to internal physical, can you go from physical to *chi*? This means can you go from paying attention to the physical parts of your body to paying attention to the energy and movement they create? Can you go from paying attention to yourself to paying attention to your partner/opponent? Can you pay attention to the area around you? Can you make your mind bigger than your body?

This is playing the space. 6-directional power. Your mind goes to the front and back, right and left, up and down.

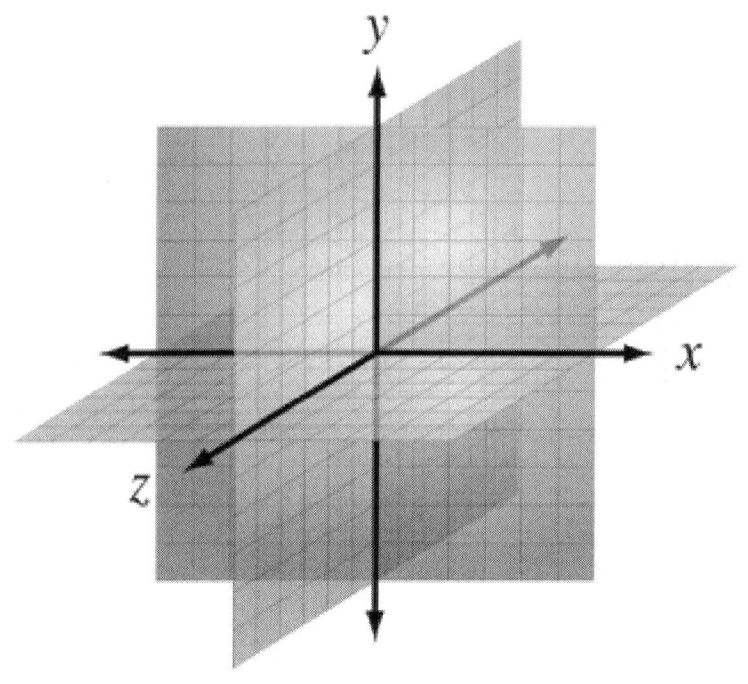

From Wikipedia

Playing the space means that you are able to see where your opponent has power, balance, and direction and then position your power, balance, and direction in a way to messes up your opponents.

You learn to read where they are weak, and then you hang out there. You separate your internal from your external so you can give the illusion of having external force, because that's what your opponent will attack and fight.

Then you attack with your internal force, while keeping them distracted and focused on your external force.

This is why we try to keep our internal force weak, that way the opponent is tricked into thinking they are winning when in reality they are being out-positioned.

The thing is, you have to go through the steps. Transform your body, then transform your energy, then transform your focus, then transform your awareness.

If you look at the early works of Monet and Van Gogh, they were realism. It took a long time for both of them to begin playing space.

Our objective is to accomplish the following things with your body:

1. Generate as much force as possible.
2. Keep your power kinetic (moving) as long as possible.
3. Only allow force to happen when you are actually hitting the target you want to hit.

To do this, you have to be tricky. This is where we get to our use of tactics.

1. Disguise the technique you are using.
2. Disguise the range from which you can attack.

3. Disguise when you will attack.
Can you use your body in the opposite way from how most people do? How far can you take this?

In this book I would not only like to go over how to build pure internal power, I would also like to discuss what to do with it. We will go from becoming pure internal to tactics and techniques.

Our ultimate concept is that martial art is the art of the predator. How does a tiger move its body. How does a tiger think? How does a tiger fight? Does a tiger think about its structure? Think about this for a moment. How can you use your body as an animal would? Your arms and legs need to be light like a wolf, your gaze as focused as a tiger, your body as powerful as a bear.

There is a fun story about the focus of a tiger. It has been said that in China, when a tiger looks at you, you become paralyzed with fear. The tiger puts its mind on you and you are trapped. The story goes that the ghost of the tiger's last victim holds you down for the tiger to eat. That person will be released, and you will become the new servant to the tiger.

This is a Wikipedia Tiger.

I don't think that is true, but there is tremendous power in focus and intention. You know the tiger wants to eat you, and it's terrifying. Can you take on this quality of focus and intention that the tiger has?

I'm not suggesting that you try to eat people. I'm suggesting that you have your mind and body so focused that it is tangible to those who see you. When you do, it is said that you have *shen*.

This means that you have 'spirit.' Your eyes become more clear, your mind is more sharp, and your awareness is much higher.

When I lived in China around the turn of the century (the most recent one) this was one of the tests that Shifu Liu would give me.

I'd do the qigong and meditation stuff that he wanted me to do that day. Then at some point in time he'd walk over to me and look into my eyes.

His wife, who I was told to call Shemu, would always say "*yo shen ma?*" "Does he have *shen*?" For 8 months the answer was "*bu shi.*"

Which of course means no. Then one day.....I passed. It took a while.

But, I'm of the opinion that time is going to go by anyway; you may as well do something constructive with it.

You'll see a lot of stuff with this whole set of ideas that is nonsense. Basically, you'll see people trying to use *chi* and *shen* to develop telekinetic abilities.

I have never met, nor seen, anyone who is telekinetic. This does not mean that *chi* and *shen* are not real. They are. But I see no evidence to support telekinesis. They are something else.

With that said, there are some awfully interesting things that we are capable of. You see people who play sports develop a sixth sense of danger around them or knowing where their teammates are without even looking.

Most people can sense if they are being looked at with intent.

This is all *shen*. It can be developed with training.

With all of this said, there are really only five things to get right in order to develop internal power. This doesn't mean that you'll know what to do with them, but it's a start.

The other two sections of this book we'll go into that. With a good teacher, it should take you about 3 or 4 years of training to get this material, and then a whole lot more to get rid of it, i.e. to master it.

BODY SPONSORSHIP: HOW TO MOVE

Body sponsorship is the concept of how to generate as much power in movement as possible. It is the process of how to have your entire body sponsor each movement, so it is never just your arm punching- it is your whole body from the feet up.

This is a phrase that I was first exposed to by Ernie Kirk, my Krav Maga instructor. I don't know if he coined the phrase or if he learned it somewhere. I asked him one time, and he thought I was crazy for asking, so wherever he got it from, it's pretty engrained for him.

There are five primary concepts to take note of:

1. Body rotation (spiraling power)
2. Shifting your weight
3. Being explosive
4. Being relaxed
5. Footwork

Body rotation is just what it sounds like it is, rotate your body. In Chinese this is called *Chan Ssu Chin*, or 'silk reeling force.' Standing still and sticking your arm out isn't good enough, you need more power. This rotation must come from the feet and hips.

To get this right, think of how a boxer would move. The body rotates, but with direction and with purpose. The big idea is to get the bulk of your body mass moving behind your technique. Remember, more mass is more power and more acceleration is more power.

- Have your weight a little bit more on your toes so you can lift your heels.
- Punch from weight. This means that one of your legs will naturally have more weight on it. Transfer your weight from one leg to the next to generate power in your punches.
- Drive your weighted leg into the ground to add more power in your punch.
- Rotate your body from the feet all the way up to the hips and shoulders.

Ultimately, after you can do that, just pay attention to your core, empty your shoulders, arms, and legs.

- Let you rear end become your new shoulder. This is key; I'll write a section on just this in a bit.
- Empty your shoulders.
- Empty your legs, especially your knees.

And of course, footwork. Move your feet to get you where you want to go. Most commonly, you would step with the leg that is closest to where you want to go and have the other leg follow.

Also, consider the predator theory. This is a phrase coined by George Xu.

One of his basic ideas is in the title of one of his video series, "Martial Art in the Art of the Predator." Your body should be light, but loose. Relaxed, but mobile. Agile, but strong.

FOOTWORK AND BALANCE

If you can't move, you can't fight. And if you can't keep your balance, you're pretty useless too.

The basic rule with footwork is that first, if you find yourself in a position where your balance is off and you can't step, then you are in trouble.

When moving, you need to get good at taking a lead step. Your key movement is always a jab, backfist, or some kind of front hand punch.

To do this you absolutely must be able to do a lead foot step to cover the ground.

To do this, the basic rule of footwork is to step with the leg closest to the direction you are going and then the other foot does a follow-up step.

No big steps. Footwork should be reasonably small so you don't sacrifice your balance for too long.

Next, to keep your balance your head should never go past your feet.

This will help you step in any direction. You must be able to move like a cat. Be light, but powerful. Be able to advance, retreat, sidestep, turn, or take angles at will.

ZHONG DING POWER: NOBODY CAN MOVE ME

Zhong Ding Jing can be translated as "central equilibrium force" and is an important part of how to use your body. My definition of this is probably not quite orthodox, but it works for me. Basically, *Zhong*

Ding is really just how to use your body to transfer force through your body into the ground.

There are a few things that define this quality:

- ☐ *Balance.*
- ☐ *Fa Song, or Melting.*
- ☐ *Touch my hand and feel my foot.*
- ☐ *Ground reaction force.*

If you read my last book, which I'm sure you didn't, it is almost completely about this topic. Being what I like to think of as an occasionally selling author, my feelings aren't hurt if you didn't pick up the last book-- but you really should.

It's funnier than this one and gives a lot of really good background information. In fact, putting together that book led me on the path of understanding that made this book possible.

Anyway, let's break down these aspects of *Zhong Ding Jing*.

If you see somebody demonstrating these qualities, it means that they are very good at using their bones, ligaments and tendons, they are good at melting, and they are good at directing energy to the ground.

Even though this isn't internal, it is extremely important. In fact, *Zhong Ding Jing* is the primary defense you have.

I say this because this give you the ability to send all of your opponent's power into the earth, meaning that you absorb very little of whatever they are doing.

And this brings us right into our first topic.

"There are five reasons for the success in fighting: first your strongest points to attack his main weaknesses; second, use your gravity against his effort; third, use your scientific against his non-scientific; fourth, use your intelligence, fake and real at the same time, against his true reaction or absence of reaction; fifth, use your maximum mind energy against his physical."

George Xu

FA SONG

Fa Song is often translated as "melting" or "relaxing." This of course is about relaxing your body in order to be able to perform internal martial arts. Both definitions are right, but as with all translations, a little bit wrong. Referencing an article written by Scott Phillips (http://northstarmartialarts.com/blog1/2007/7/30/what-does-song-mean.html?rq=song)

As well as the teachings of George Xu, *song* can be likened to a pine cone opening. Or if you live in my neck of the woods, like a Christmas tree flopping open.

I follow Scott Phillips' blog at NorthStarMartialArts.com. He thinks about this differently than I do, he has different references from his life experience, and he's not afraid to share an unorthodox thought.

I have a great deal of respect for him. I especially enjoy his theories on the origin of the Chen Tai Chi form. But don't tell him I said that; it'll go to his head.

Anyway, back to our analogy. A lot of times when you buy a Christmas tree, they wrap it up in a net to make it easier to transport.

When you get home and prop the tree up, you then have to cut the net off. When you do of course it flops open. You want to be like that.

The idea is that you don't wilt onto the ground, rather you relax and open yourself. Your skeleton stays upright and your muscles relax.

Relax your neck and shoulders. Relax your chest and back. Relax your waist and hips. Especially relax the psoas muscles.

This really gives the sense of centeredness and "openingness." If that's even a word.

This concept is absolutely imperative to get right if you want to get this type of art right.

If you have any tension in your body at all, you simply cannot develop ground force nor pure internal power.

The rest of your body will get in the way.

This does require a complete paradigm shift of what you are doing with your body and even how you perceive what your body is.

As a side note, if you Google *Fa Song* you get an Otis Redding song.

While we're talking about people in the martial arts community that I respect, we must of course also mention Dr. Susan Matthews.

Again, her perspective on martial arts in general is very different from mine. She shares Scott's love for dance, while I mostly like to hit things.

DUSTIN BRADFORD / Special to the Herald

Susan has had great results with teaching her students to fill themselves with white light from the top of the head down. She has an entire routine that she took me through last year that is great.

You begin by closing your eyes and relaxing. Then you picture having light come into the top of your head. Let the light fill your head with a cleansing and healing idea.

Then let the light work its way down into your neck, filling outward with cleansing energy.

Then down to your shoulders and chest, same cleansing energy. Be mindful to not let energy get stuck in your heart. Keep it flowing.

Then your belly and waist. Then hips. Then legs. Filling your entire body with light, energy, and relaxed cleansing. Let this then touch the ground. Connect with the ground, and then let your energy go into the ground, from there accept the energy from the ground back up into yourself in a pillar of light and good stuff. Have this pillar of light go all the way up into the sky.

Good stuff. As you can see, she approaches this material in a very different way than I do. Yet her thoughts are extremely educated and valuable.

She has a whole process that she does with this that is very effective and is unique. If I recall correctly, she calls her method "Spiral Anatomy."

Susan is one of those smart people that you would do well to look into.

I've taken classes in various disciplines where they attempt this, but those instructors are lacking something Susan has, the Dr. in front of her name.

Her Doctorate is in Neuroscience, which she pursued with the express purpose of applying an advanced knowledge of Neuroscience to Tai Chi.

Visit her site online and get some of her videos. She's worth it.

4 BECOMES 1

This is a pretty simple idea that seems complicated at first. The basic notion is that you want your core body mass-- your butt and torso-- to be what you think of as moving when you move, and the limbs need to be empty but attached.

How do you do this? With your serratus and adductor muscles. Simple. More on this in a minute.

This is often explained as joining all of your limbs into the middle of your body, also called *nei dan* Power, or the "eternal pearl.'

The idea is that you pull your adductor muscles inside of your legs up and your serratus muscles down and badda boom badda bing they go to the middle of your body.

I think many if not most texts on internal martial arts confuse *nei dan* and *dan tien*. The *nei dan*, Internal Pearl, is the point where you think of your limbs attaching- as mentioned above. The *dan tien* is the Elixir Pool, or field of cinnabar.

In the 6 Steps to Self Mastery I go into this in more detail- but basically the *dan tien* is the circle in the middle of your body that does all of your movement-- the gluteus maximus, the psoas, the oblique, and the diaphragm.

Again, more on this later.

The *nei dan* is one point inside of the *dan tien*, but they serve different functions.

When you read a book saying that the *dan tien* is a single point in the middle of the body they are confusing the *dan tien* with the *nei dan* and then probably confusing the *wuji* point in there somewhere as well.

This is a common image of a Daoist Adept. What does that mean? That varies. Basically it's a dude who's really into Daoism. What does that mean? Nothing, don't worry about it. Just live your life, be calm, be centered and go with the flow. Relax buddy-- look a seagull.

The *wuji* point is supposedly the first cell that formed life in your body and is in the very middle of you-- right between your belly button and your tailbone.

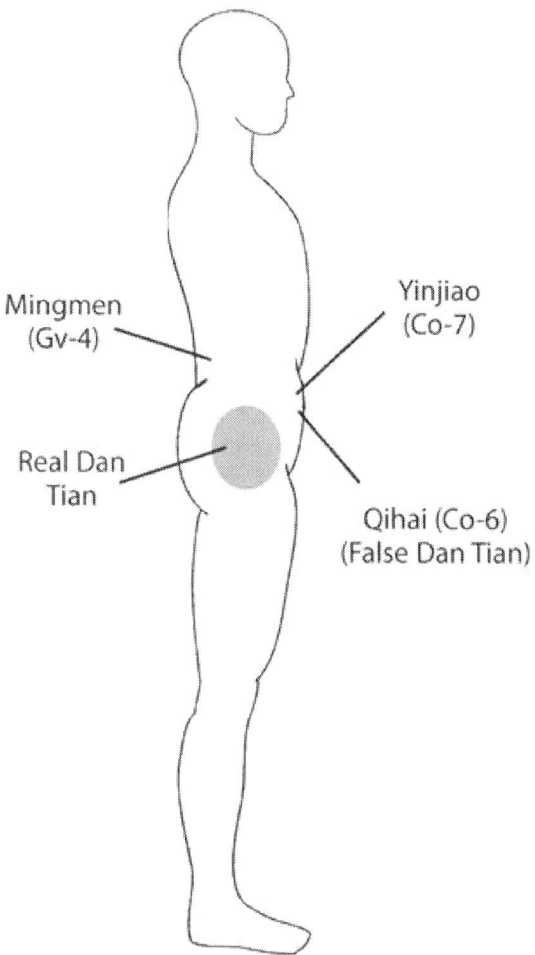

Mingmen
(Gv-4)

Yinjiao
(Co-7)

Real Dan
Tian

Qihai (Co-6)
(False Dan Tian)

By the way, this picture is incomplete. The *dan tien* should be bigger, from the bottom of the rib cage down to the gluteus maximus.

Some of the old Chinese Masters even theorized that the *wuji* point was an actual physical thing that was a ball in the middle of your belly.

I'm not so sure about that, and I'm not so sure about the first cell thing either, but it's a pretty theory if you like it.

And after all, as Obi Wan said, many of the truths we cling to are from a certain point of view.

This is an old Chinese dude for your enjoyment. I figured I'd be sued for putting in a picture of Obi Wan, and George Lucas would probably not be the guy to deliver the notice. So here is a substitute. Pretend he is a Jedi. Do it for me.

SHOULDERS AND PUNCHING

Now let's look at this thinking specifically about movement.

Let's start with this pertaining to your arms and legs. Something Bill Wallace teaches stands out here as the best description I've come across for this.

He describes how to use your shoulder for throwing a jab and how to use your leg for throwing a kick.

First, the key principle is that muscles are binary. All muscles contract or relax. On your arm you have your biceps to bend your elbow and your triceps to straighten your arm.

If you are trying to bend your arm and there is tension in your triceps, you will be slower and weaker because you are fighting yourself. You should just relax your triceps and use your biceps.

One of the things that George Xu always says is that you should not use your shoulder. Bill Wallace says this as well.

They are from different disciplines, but they have several similarities of thought-- here is one.

If you lift your shoulder to punch, your arm is no longer backed up by the rest of the body. Keep your shoulder down so your arm has superior backup body mass.

Also if you tense up the front of the deltoid to lift your arm you give away when you are going to punch; you still lose back up body mass, and you are fighting yourself; thus you are slower.

Instead, keep the shoulder down and use the Serratus Anterior to connect the arm to the torso, then use your triceps to extend your arm with your biceps and front of your shoulder relaxed.

To lift your arm, use the first half of a parabolic arc or you may think of it as a hyperbolic arc instead of just lifting it straight up. This means that your arm should come up and then go out from the vertex.

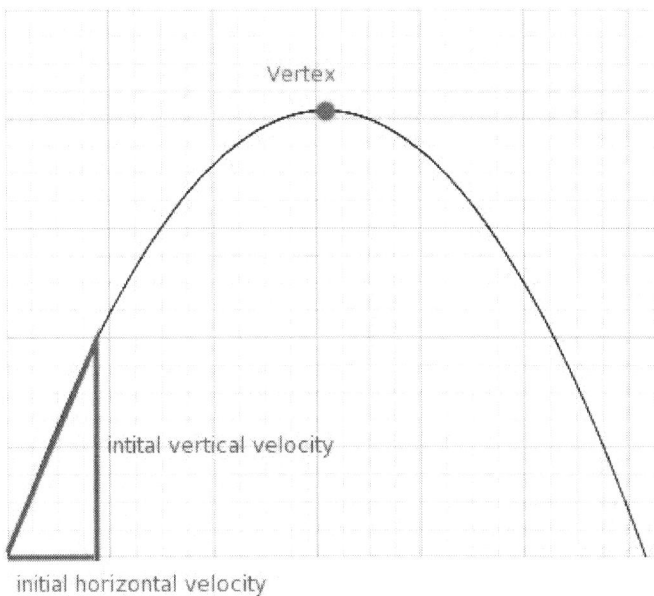

You're going to have to play with this to get it right, but when you figure it out this will be life altering.

Lifting your arm is actually very similar to doing bent over dumbbell rows. Use your back to lift the dumbbell, use your back to lift your fist.

Figure 4
http://www.fitnessandpower.com/training/workout-routines/how-to-perform-barbell-dumbbell-bent-over-rows-with-proper-form

This will give you connection to body mass, speed, and therefore more power.

Serratus Anterior

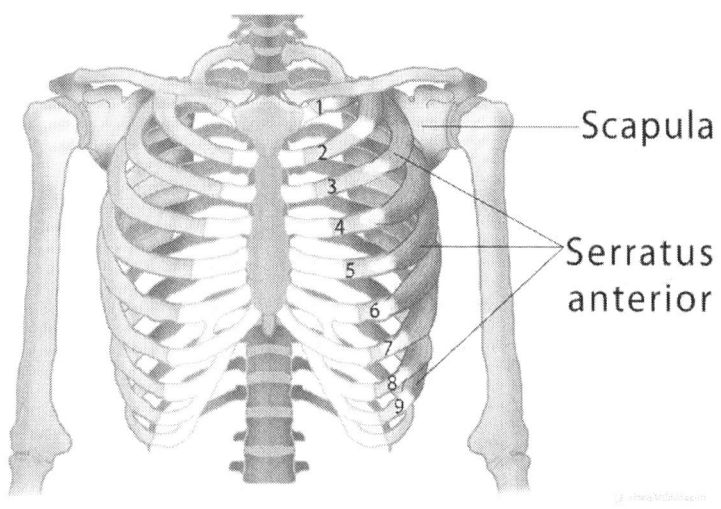

Scapula

Serratus anterior

Wikipedia again. This is what you use to stabilize your arm and attach it to the rest of your body. This way you have more of your body supporting your arm. Also, force entering your arm goes into the ground. If the force goes into your shoulder, traps and neck, you get lifted up and go off balance.

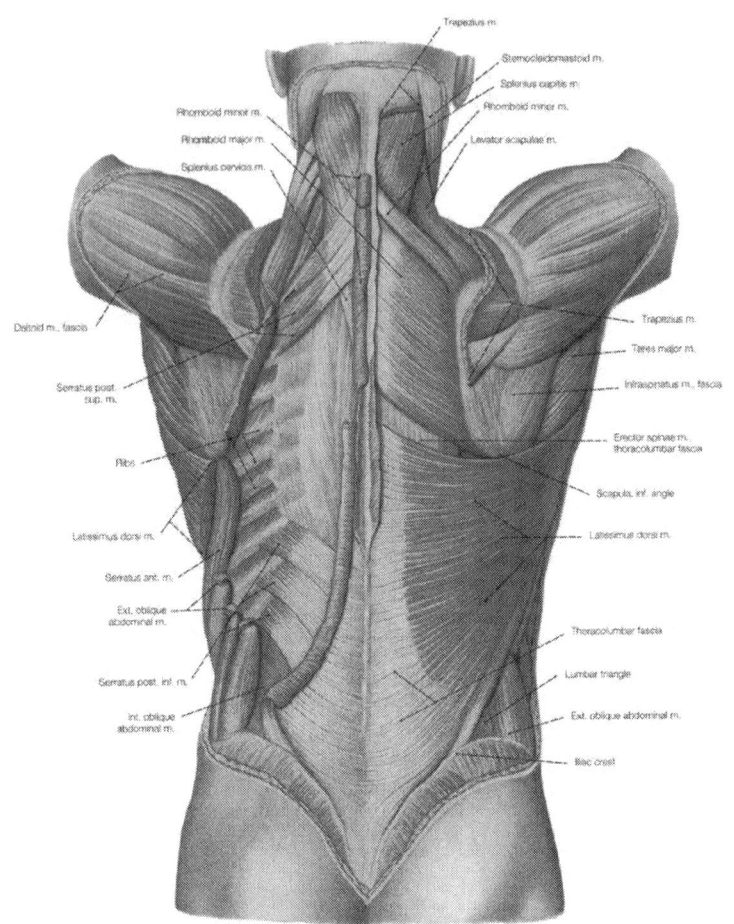

Wikipedia Picture.

You should punch with your shoulder empty, but connected through your serratus and the back of your armpit. Think about how a tiger or a wolf uses its torso to move, not the shoulder. It's more relaxed, efficient, powerful, and sustainable than using the shoulder.

HIPS AND KICKING

Now on to the legs. This part is kinda tricky. As always, you only want to use the muscles you need; the other ones get in the way and slow you down.

We'll talk about kicking and then go into the hips, or the *kua* as we like to call it in Chinese.

For kicking you need to use your adductor muscles to move your leg and keep everything else relaxed until you need them.

The real trick is, as always, only use the muscles that do the work you want done and have all other muscles relaxed.

I really, really like the Superfoot system of kicking. Bill Wallace uses the same internal qualities that George Xu teaches, only he does it with kicking and boxing.

At one time it was hypothesized that there was no way to do internal kicking and nobody who could do it.

The thing is, the Chinese systems are really not good at kicking. Not as good as the Japanese, Korean, and American methods. And this is coming from a guy who loves Chinese Martial Arts. To me they combine the mystery of the Jedi Knights, Caradine's Kung Fu, and Batman's Vision Quest all in one. But they stink at kicking.

Turns out, Bill Wallace has Internal kicking.

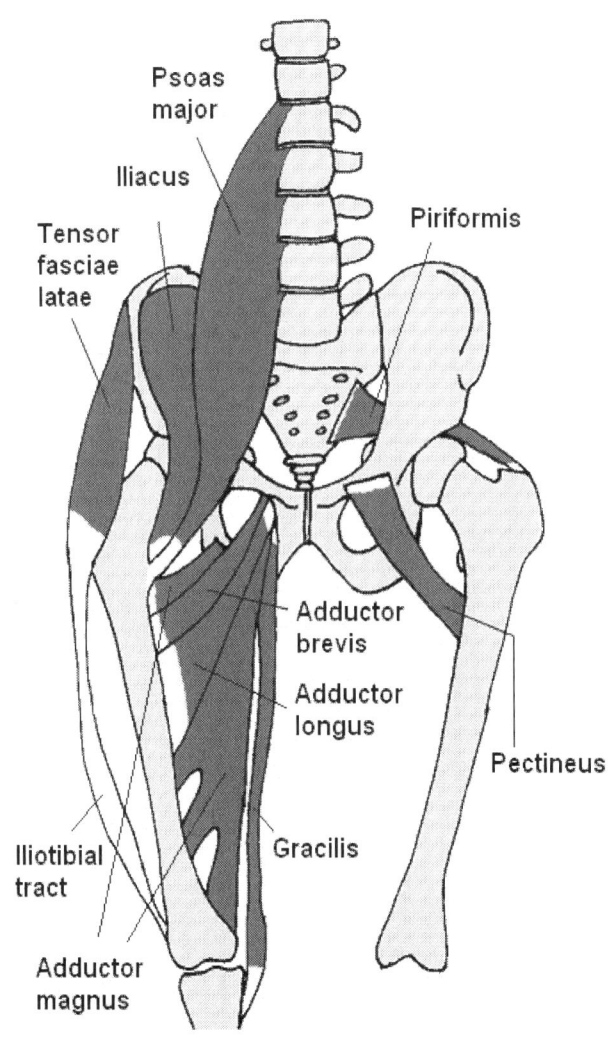

Psoas major

Iliacus

Tensor fasciae latae

Piriformis

Adductor brevis

Adductor longus

Pectineus

Iliotibial tract

Gracilis

Adductor magnus

This wiki-image is hugely important, it shows most of the muscles you need to have good internal anything.

For example, you'll use your quadriceps to do a round kick, and your hamstring to do a hook kick, but don't use those until you are actually doing the kick.

Think of a side kick as doing a squat. If you drive your foot into the ground to lift something you are using mostly your rear end and quadriceps.

Wikipedia Image

Again, it is not difficult to kick high enough for most people. The problem is rarely actual flexibility, it is more often a lack of strength and a lack of relaxation.

As with the shoulder, you should relax the muscles that do not do the work you want.

Bill Wallace talks about how most of the time when people tell him they are inflexible it is really more that they are unable to relax and therefore they fight themselves with every motion. That's why they feel like the tin man.

So when you work on flexibility, you really are working on relaxing specific parts of your body.

The hips are referred to as the *kua* in Chinese. As always, relax everything.

Relax the hip Tensor, relax the Piriformis as well as the Pectineus, and let your lower back relax.

This is important when we get to the internal power part of the show.

Also, for kicking you need to relax the back of your leg. The leg bicep can flap in the breeze for all we care. And your calf also needs to be empty and relaxed. Your foot is relaxed, but holds its shape. When you kick just think about your rear end and your knee as a pivot point. Everything else is dead weight.

This will make you fast and powerful. Think about it. Your leg weighs roughly 1/3 of your body weight. I weigh 200 pounds. Wanna get hit in the head with a 67 pound dead weight? Me neither.

For now think about this as making sure you have good range of motion in the hips and a stable, low center of gravity.

Tight hips make your footwork as well as kicking bad. Work on it.

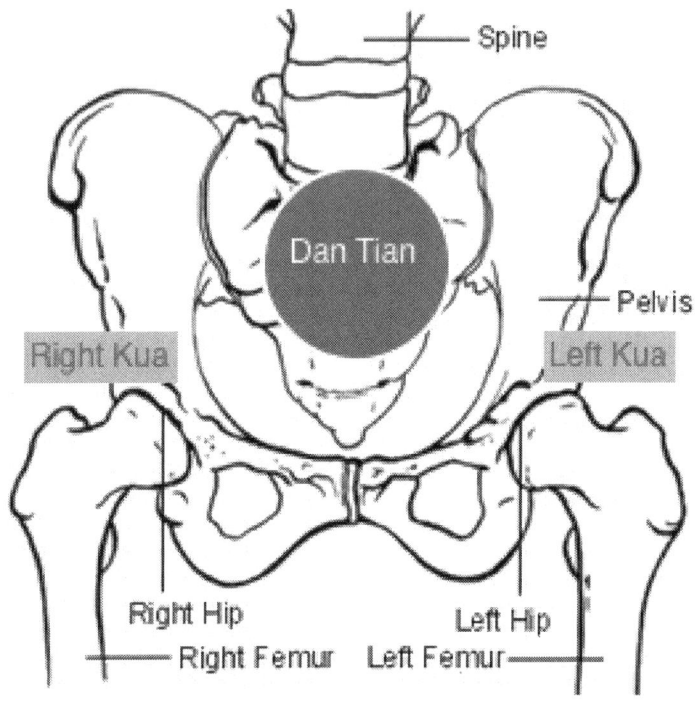

From http://kung-fu.co.za/tag/three-dantians/. This is a good display of the *kua*. They've confused the *dan tien* with the *nei dan*, but don't worry about that. In order to move your hips correctly for Martial Art, Boxing, and other sports you need to be able to fold relax, open, and fold the *kua*. This allows free movement as well as freeing up the Psoas for centering and sinking your *chi*.

You get range of motion as well as access to the power muscle groups.

TOUCH MY HAND AND FEEL MY FOOT

This is a concept that we use as our main defensive tactic.

What this means is that when your opponent makes contact with you, you need to automatically send that power to the ground.

This does two things:

1. Your opponent is tricked because they think your power is in your arm, when you are

actually sending it down and they are touching the ground.

2. Your chance for injury goes down.
3. Your opponent is pinned in one spot for the time that they are touching you.
4. Your internal power is still free and is not bound to your hand technique.

This is a separate system from the internal. First, your hand technique (punch, chop, or whatever) is real. It uses all of the things we've discussed so far.

However, it is also a trap and a trick. More on this later. We want to layer your techniques and tactics. For this level, think about all of the techniques you have learned thus far. The style doesn't matter.

You still have punches chops, hammer fists, elbows, and whatever else. Then you have them in various combinations and sequences. Most fighters tend to have about 5 combinations that they throw.

So there should be traps within the techniques themselves, but the fact that there is a technique is also a trap because we actually want to attack with internal power.

INTERNAL POWER: NOBODY CAN OVERPOWER ME

This is a big one. Eventually, we want to have purely and only internal power. We want the internal to go first and before your technique.

So first, we have to define what internal power is. I find that the vast majority, and I mean vast, of people professing to teach internal power are simply wrong about the definition.

You first have to become clear on what is what.

Internal power is the use of the diaphragm and muscles under your bottom ribs, iliopsoas process, and the erector spinae.

You can look at the picture to see what this means.

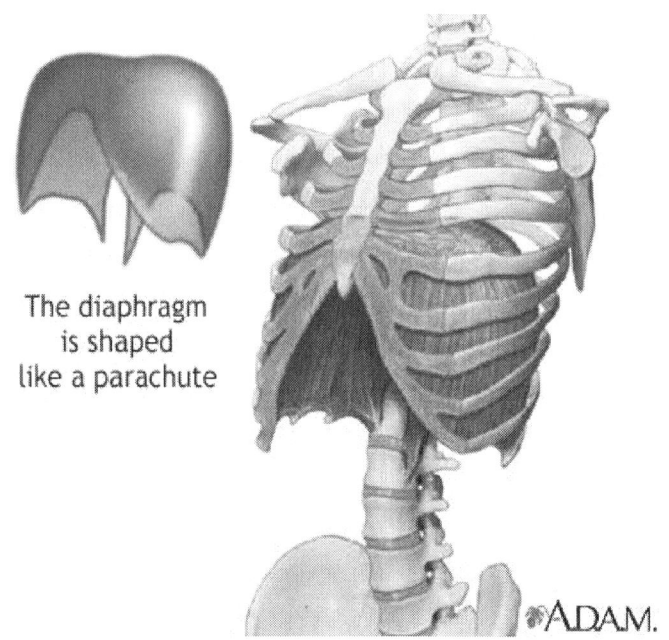

The diaphragm is shaped like a parachute

The diaphragm is of course generally related to breathing. Believe it or not, we need to think about breathing as a separate system than the internal. More on that later.

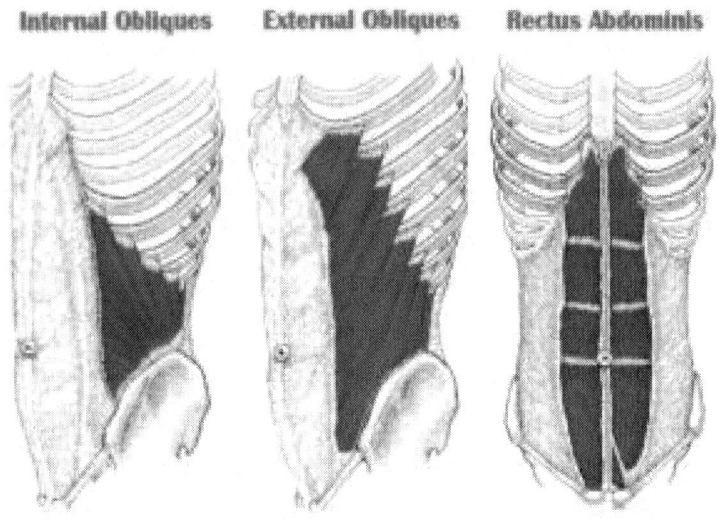

You need to be able to move your lower rib cage around to give direction to the force your body is creating.

In class I say that you move your diaphragm to move your bottom ribs up, down, and diagonally.

What I really mean is that we want to think of moving the lower rib cage.

There are all kinds of muscles involved in this, but if you think of the diaphragm moving then you will have the correct movement of the lower rib cage.

Your rib cage needs to move up and down with some diagonal movement as well as you are generating force.

If you try to lift the shoulders up from the top of your rib cage the arms become separate from the rest of your body mass and you lose all of your power.

However, your rib cage does have to be able to move and change position, so you lift and move it from the bottom. This way you have the mobility you need, and still have the connection to mass and power.

Next, is your rear end.

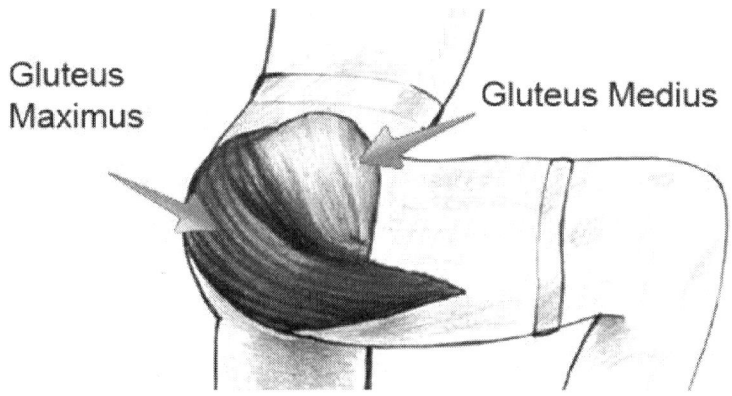

Gluteus Maximus

Gluteus Medius

Your glutes are important for movement of the hip and thigh and are regarded as some of the strongest muscles on your body.

In terms of hand techniques, *think of your buttocks as your new shoulder*. What I mean by this is exactly what I just said.

Think about your rear end as your shoulder. Use it to move everything.

Think about it this way. Your buttocks are mostly for things like squatting, lunging, getting up out of chairs, walking, and anything else that extends the leg.

What if you push your rear end down in a fashion similar to squatting, only you don't quite actually squat.

This gives your body the upward power of doing a squat, but with mobility. I often phrase this as "push your butt down."

If you push your buttocks down while at the same time moving your diaphragm you create a very strong up and down power. Learn to use this to power all of your physical movement.

You will become close to unstoppable.

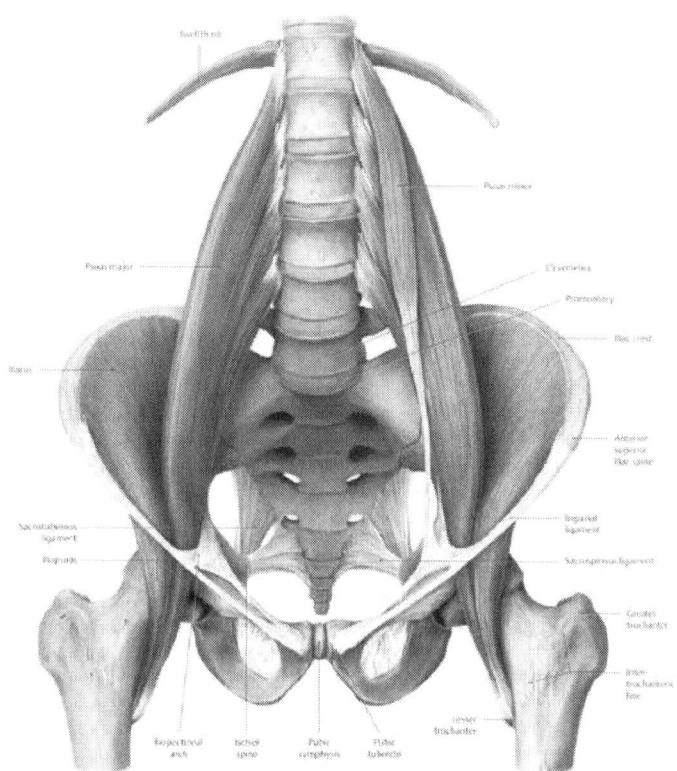

The Iliacus and psoas muscles are important stabilizers for walking, running, standing, and so on.

They really help hold everything in the middle of your body together.

The iliopsoas also rotates the thigh laterally.

A lot of fitness gurus will talk about how important and magical the psoas is. They aren't wrong.

When you figure out how to relax this area of your body your center of gravity drops and you become much more stable.

Earlier I mentioned the *kua*. By my definition this is specifically the V of the hips.

Obviously, this area is greatly affected by how you use the iliacus and psoas, as well as the hip tensor.

Relax all of these.

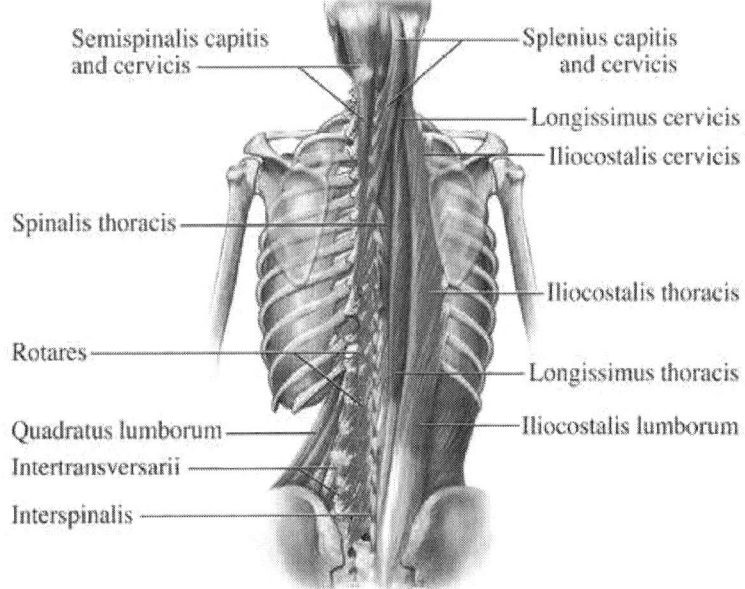

And last but not least, the spine. Do not think of your spine as a post, rather think of it as a snake.

Something that is alive and can shrink and expand.

Your spine holds up your entire body, but it is also the basis for your movement. A key element to proper use of the spine is to relax the lumbar curve of the lower back.

This allows energy to travel downward through your body and not get stuck in your chest.

What you do is think of these muscles as making a sphere right in the middle of your body that can stretch up and down like an accordion, with spiraling movement, lateral movement, and diagonal movement.

All at the same time:

- Your buttocks press down,
- Your diaphragm lifts up and rotates your rib cage towards your opponent,
- Your lower back relaxes and your lumbar curve does not curve forward, and
- Your iliopsoas muscles relax to offer a lower center of gravity as well as side stability.

This creates the expanding *dan tien* effect that is necessary for there to be internal power.

Dan tien is a word used to refer to the middle of your body, it is your "elixir pool." I go into a bit of detail about this in the last book.

For our purposes here, suffice it to say that the *dan tien* is the sphere created by the shrinking and expanding feeling created through the spherical use of the muscles described in here.

Ultimately, you want these movements, your *dan tien*, to be how you do everything. Move from here.

Most people who exercise purpose driven movement like boxers, kickboxers, grapplers, tennis players, and swimmers have internal power.

If you do something where you practice still postures, stances, and poses, it is unlikely that your internal power is very good.

These people may or may not have good internal strength to hold a pose, but that is not what we are looking for. We are looking for the ability to use the internal muscles to perform tasks that involve variability.

There are really four things you can do with internal power.

1. Arm technique goes first, there is no internal power relative to movement.
2. Arm technique goes first, with the internal power behind it. This is more powerful, but if somebody blocks your arm they stop your

entire body and you have to completely abandon your position to try again.

3. Internal power goes first, followed by the arm technique. This is good as the arm technique can be blocked and your body is still progressing with the attack.

4. Internal power attacks where your opponent has no balance, structure, or kinetic energy goes towards you, your arm technique is next. This is even better, as you are now using your maximum power against where your opponent has nothing.

I am getting a bit ahead of myself with these as you will read more about this in a later section, but reading it here can't hurt too much.

Like I said, you want to get so good at internal movement and dexterity that you can use internal power to do everything.

Read the following quote from George and think about what he is saying. This is pretty heavy stuff. The Predator Theory states that not only are you always pure internal, you also have a few other things going on. We'll try to cover these.

"Then you have to put these qualities in "nobody knows me, I know you" situation plus light and heavy, soft and hard, fake and real at the same time. Use a scientific way, a 3 dimension spiral power plus borrow enemy action (shi) force to create your comfortable, maximum and superior shi to attack his empty and weakest points. Plus your mind spiritual is tiger hunting the human, the Olympic spirit competition to get the maximum."

George Xu

GRAVITY POWER: NOBODY CAN LIFT ME

George Xu would say that your opponent should carry you, do not carry yourself. This is also called *na jing*, or 'controlling power.'

Remember, George's PhD is in math. So he's talking about gravity in reference to the idea of gravity relative to the General Theory of Relativity.

As a refresher, Wikipedia says,

"Gravity is most accurately described by the general theory of relativity (proposed by Albert Einstein in 1915) which describes gravity not as a force, but as a consequence of the curvature of spacetime caused by the uneven distribution of mass/energy. The most extreme example of this curvature of spacetime is a black hole, from which nothing can escape once past its event horizon, not even light.[1] More gravity results in gravitational time dilation, where time lapses more slowly at a lower (stronger) gravitational potential. However, for most applications, gravity is well approximated by Newton's law of universal gravitation, which describes gravity as a force which causes any two bodies to be attracted to each other, with the force proportional to the product of their masses and inversely proportional to the square of the distance between them."

George also defines gravity in this context as giving your opponent your entire relaxed body. You don't do anything, you are relaxed and give your entire mass to your opponent.

This does not mean to lean on your opponent.

Your opponent must feel your gravity, while if they break contact with you, you are completely on balance, just completely melted.

Gravity in this context is a function of a few different things working together.

- Focus on your opponent, not yourself.
- Obtain a position of superior balance.
- Occupy the space your opponent is not in.

If a power lifter is picking up a weight, they have to get under it. If someone is holding a baby, there is a tendency to cock the hip sideways to be under the baby.

As we will discuss further, to make this really work you must be able to transfer your opponent's energy into the ground and not let it become force in your body.

Next, you need to have internal power and body sponsorship.

This way, you can empty your opponent's energy and give your body mass to your opponent. This means that you position your body in such a way that you have superior balance and position relative to your opponent.

You also want to use the stronger parts of your body against your opponent; thus you "take the space and balance from your opponent."

Their force is dumped into the ground, which also effectively roots them so they can't move, while the bulk of your body force is attacking them.

Figure 5 Zulfiya Chinshanlo, World Champion 2009 in the 53kg class performing the jerk portion of the lift. Look at how she's under the weight, her arms are attached into her torso, and though at the moment of this picture she's stuck on her front quadracep, I'll bet she fixes that in a hurry and stabilizes that weight through herself onto the ground.

The difference between lifting and holding something and martial art is that we need to be able to generate superior position from any direction at any angle.

The first thing to consider is your body position.

Have your weight slightly forward on the balls of your feet.

Have your hips slightly folded.

Have your focus on your opponent. Shoulders relaxed. Just like a tennis player in fact.

Next, consider your opponent's position.

Where is the center of gravity, where is the structure in the legs, and where is the incoming force?

We call this 6-directional power. It means that no matter where the incoming energy is coming from, you need to be able to direct it wherever you want to without turning it into force. Remember, force is where there is a transfer of energy. You don't want somebody else's energy turning to force in your body; that's how we break things.

Look at this picture of a tennis player. She is in a solid yet mobile athletic position so she can go any direction. She is prepared to go anywhere to get the ball and can do so quickly and on balance.

What we want to do is not so different.

She plays tennis. http://tennisfixation.com/how-to-use-the-tennis-ready-position-tennis-quick-tips-podcast-31.html

SPACE POWER AND *SHI*: YOU DON'T KNOW ME, BUT I KNOW YOU

George has talked about s*hi* for years. He would say, "this is *shi.* " And then Judo Chop the fool out of somebody. By the way, this is funny because Judo has no chops. Don't worry, he never hurts anybody.

Don't missunderestimate me.

From what I've been told, this is rather unique for a traditional Chinese Martial Arts Instructor.

Back in the day, as early as 30 years ago, and in all reality probably still today, asking a question of your teacher could be a life-threatening experience.

George Xu has a story of a friend of his who asked a question of his teacher and the teacher killed him demonstrating the answer. Fortunately, George didn't train with this teacher.

Probably for the best, as George has an inquisitive mind.

Remember, force is where a transfer of energy takes place, kinetic energy is where something has energy and is moving through space, and potential energy is where something has the possibility of moving but hasn't yet.

Force is *jing*. Jing is where there is a transfer of energy.

Kinetic energy is *chi*. *Chi* is energy. Energy is the change is a given system.

Potential energy is *shi*. *Shi* is potential, *shi* is playing the emptiness.

Wikipedia defines Potential Energy like this:

"In physics, potential energy is energy possessed by a body by virtue of its position relative to others, stresses within itself, electric charge, and other factors."

Shi is using your body in a way that you are playing potential.

You move in such a way that your kinetic energy never transfers to force in your opponent until you want it to-- until you have struck a vital target.

At the same time you make your opponent turn to *jing* as quickly as possible.

This is the function of "touch my hand and feel my feet." You want to root your opponent.

I know a lot of martial arts talk about how rooting is a desirable thing, but I disagree.

If you can't move, you can't fight.

If you are playing football against a "rooted" defense, you are in for a good day.

Next, learn to navigate your kinetic energy, your movement, to where your opponent has no kinetic energy, no force, and no potential energy.

So you play your potential energy and your kinetic energy against your opponent's potential and kinetic energy.

Remember to use your internal power as your primary power source.

Think about your internal power as you. The entirety of your body is the internal and is moved by the internal.

Your internal power is what you are traveling through space, creating gravity with, and so on.

I like to begin teaching this with a fairly simple series of concepts.

1. Do not attack where your opponent is on balance. **The Plumb Bob Principle.**
2. Do not attack where your opponent has structure. **The A Frame Principle.**
3. Do not attack where your opponent is attacking. **The Don't be Cannon Fodder Principle.**

This is pretty self-explanatory, but let's discuss it anyway. Perhaps talking about it more will shed some light on it.

These three principles are what you look for in your opponent so you know what to attack. Basically, don't attack these three things, Attack everything else.

This way you are always putting your maximum effort into attacking their maximum weakness.

Here is a description of these three things.

THE PLUMB-BOB PRINCIPLE

A plumb-bob is a weight attached to a string designed to measure a straight downward line in carpentry. There is a whole section on this in my last book.

The plumb bob for our purposes is a way to describe central balance. If the plumb bob is tied to the very top of your head and allowed to fall straight down as if your body wasn't there, then your central equilibrium would be visible.

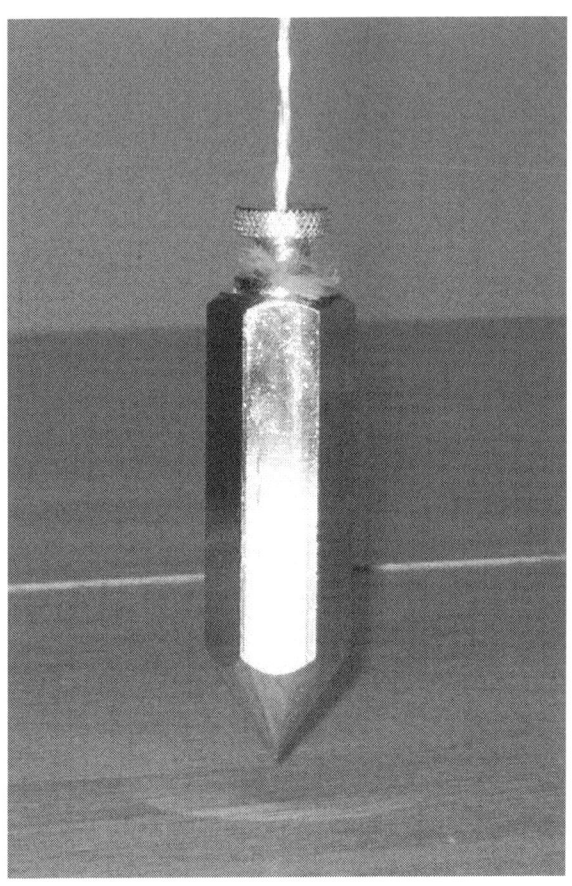

Basically, don't attack people on where they are on balance. Attack people where they are not on balance.

What is interesting about this is that you need to be able to do this while in motion. You and your opponent in motion at the same time, Learn to feel where the balance point is at all times. This way you can learn to position yourself so that you are never attacking quite where they are on balance and strong;

always attack where your opponent is off balance and weak.

Though there is nothing internal about this picture, can you see where the balance points are as they are in motion? She is balanced backwards even though she has the knife and began as the bad guy in this drill. Yes, the blue piece of pool noodle is the knife. What, you didn't think we practiced with real knives did you?

THE A-FRAME PRINCIPLE

If you think of a capital A, you will see that there are two points on the ground and one is the middle. The two points on the ground are your feet, and the point in the middle is roughly the middle of your chest.

This is where your opponent's structure is the strongest.

Do not attack them there. Instead attack where your opponent has no structure. Our basic model is that you don't attack where their stance gives them structure, but also consider how that structure will change as they move. Should you uproot this structure, go over it, go around it, or maybe blast through it?

That's up to you, but remember that you need to build in yourself an understanding of structure and where it is powerful.

This is also why we try not to directly intercept punches. We spiral them, block them, or crush there, but we try not to eat them.

Thanks Paul Mannix for the lovely picture!

THE DON'T BE CANNON FODDER PRINCIPLE

Stay out of the direct line of force generated by your opponent. If there is a fist moved towards your nose, you need to move your nose.

Also, we want to use the inverse of this concept to disguise your technique as well. Your punch going to the face of your opponent is one attack, but your main attack is your internal attacking their internal's holes and your mind attacking where they have no potential energy.

This seems like foolishly simple advice, and yet I see numerous 'Internal Martial Artists" trying to be all mystical or something and getting punched in the face. I don't know what they are thinking. I guess these people figure that if they want something enough it will happen by sheer force of their desire. Sadly, it doesn't work that way.

Thanks for the pic Smatprt. Cannon Fodder is originally from Henry the 4th, Part 1. Just fyi.

You have to learn technique, you have to learn to use your body well, you have to learn how to generate *chi* and what it is in the first place, and then you have to learn to direct all of this with your mind.

If you just skip to the mind part, it's just your imagination.

This is an image from a popular video of a Tai Chi guy vs an MMA coach. The Tai Chi guy was comically beaten.

I assume it's because he tried to meditate, do qigong, and do forms to train for a fight.

To get good at fighting you have to fight. It's funny that way, but you get good at what you train at.

Here is what all of this boils down to. *Shi* is your ability to attack where your opponent has no structure, no balance, and no energy traveling towards you. You use all of your ability to attack where they are nothing. Furthermore, you attack where they are going to have nothing.

You negate their balance, structure, and energy with superior position, technique, internal, and mind. You play the space that they are not using on an ongoing and changing level. Or if you are from my neck of the woods:

Go where they ain't, but make 'em think you're where you ain't.

"Body must not focus on the techniques. If focus on techniques then it will limit by techniques. Body must not focus on force (Jin). If focus on Jin then it will expose your structure and power directions. Body must not focus on Qi. If focus on Qi then it will stuck on Qi and lost Shi and freedom of the mind. You must have whole body harmony from physical energy to mind, from inside to outside, from movements to stillness. All of these are base on nobody knows me but I know you." (Note: Qi=Chi.)

George Xu

THE SECRET SAUCE

Here is the secret to *shi*. Are you ready? It's simple, just hard to do. It's to do with your legs. George would say that *shi* is the Buddha's Halo. Not the kind that wraps around your head, the kind that encompasses your whole body.

Your gluteus maximus and the leg biceps are the secret in conjunction with your *kua*-- loose, open, and empty hips.

Use your but, back of your legs, and hips like a crouching tiger. This is where your indirect power is. Then use the loose and empty *kua* (the V of the hips) to aim and direct the power generated by the back of the legs. This is also why you don't straighten your legs if you wish to use *shi*. Then you would lose the crouching tiger quality and go to structure.

You would like to get good enough with this quality that you can use it to control your opponent completely. Just by touching you, your opponent is completely in your control as you are controlling the entire space around them.

George says the way he discovered this is that he was jetlagged and dead tired while teaching in Italy. He had some big dude pushing on him doing a body quality test, and George just had nothing left to offer. So he completely melted and found that he could just have all of his force come from his haunches.

Use the back of your legs, and then use freedom in your hips to aim where the power goes, after that attack with your gravity, then your internal, and last is the technique.

Don't tell anybody I told you this.

PUTTING IT ALL TOGETHER

To recap, here are the important things that you are working with to generate power and position.

1. **Body Sponsorship-** *Jing*
   a. Always punch from the transition of your weight.
   b. Use spiraling power from the feet and hips that you then express into your striking.
   c. Be relaxed.
2. **Zhong Ding** *Jing*

a. Be relaxed, only the use the muscles that do the job you are trying to do, relax the other muscles.

b. Use the Serratus and Oblique muscles to attach your arms to your body mass.

c. Relax your lower back and think of your spine as a single living organism.

d. All of this enables you to transfer all of your opponent's energy into the ground, not into you.

e. This is your defense.

3. **Pure Internal Power-** *Dan Tien*

a. Use the buttocks as you shoulder.

b. Use the buttocks, diaphragm, and psoas to create a sphere in the middle of your body.

c. Use this sphere to create up and down force that can be adjusted to fit what you want.

d. Internal power becomes pure internal power when you use it for everything, disregarding every other part of your body.

e. Internal Power leaves the body when you press your tailbone towards your target.

4. **Gravity Power**

a. Your opponent carries you, you do not carry yourself.
b. Use body sponsorship, *zhong ding*, as well as internal power to create superior body position relative to your opponent.
c. Find where you opponent does not have:
   i. Balance relative to their plumb bob.
   ii. Structure relative to their A frame.
   iii. Directional force coming at you.
   iv. The intention of direction.
d. Use your body position and internal to fill in the space where your opponent has nothing, sabotaging their balance as well as potential movement.

5. **Space Power- *Shi***
   a. Learn to play potential energy.
      i. Put your potential energy and intention where your opponent has none.
   b. Ignore yourself, ignore your opponent, be where you are not and be where your opponent is not.
   c. Be only mind energy.
      i. Learn your techniques, tactics, and how to use your body so well that

you don't need to pay attention to yourself.

The basic tactic of internal martial arts is

1. Learn your martial arts techniques and tactics. Master them. Body sponsorship is part of this.
2. Use *zhong ding* power to disguise your power and trick your opponent into thinking your main power is somewhere it is not.
3. Separate your internal power from your *zhong ding* power. Use internal power to continue and create motion against your opponent different than the technique of your arm.
4. Try to put your internal where your opponent has nothing.

This means that you are attacking on different planes and different levels. Your technique, for example your punch, is real and is attacking in one place.

When contact occurs, your opponent blocks your punch, your internal continues and is not attached to the technique.

At the same time, the technique sends your opponent's power to the earth and not into you. This does not root you, you can still move, this roots your opponent.

Your internal continues to attack where your opponent is weakest. This is where they have no balance, no structure, and no energy nor force directed at you.

You need to be able to change as your opponent changes. Like a dragon swimming in the clouds. Your opponent doesn't know where the dragon is, even if they know it is there they can't find it.

Just like this the opponent's balance is gone before they even realize it, before there is even contact with you.

If they cannot stop your technique, you crush them. If they stop your technique, you crush them.

If they are too hard, they are broken. If they are too soft, they are destroyed.

You strike like lightning, only when your opponent is off balance and broken.

Only then do you put your body mass behind technique.

Only then does your opponent know that they are finished, only when it is too late.

Your mind is power and your body is empty. Your eyes see all and your power is unstoppable.

You are the hidden dragon.

You are the unstoppable tiger.

Move like a tiger, move like a predator.

You are light but powerful, you are empty and vast, you are focused and aware. Patient, yet explosive.

You are power disguised.

George has decided to call his art *Ling Cong Shen Shi Men*, or 'Empty Body in Space Mind Energy Style.'

This actually a pretty good name for what he does as he wants his style to be about mind energy operating freeing in space.

To quote George on the subject from his website, *ling* is 'traveling.'

Kong is 'empty in space.' My force is traveling in the space.

Shen is 'spiritual, mental.'

Shi is 'potential, invisible, indirect force.' *Shi* is not *jing*."

On http://www.susanamatthews.com/taichi-secrets.htm.

The object of this is to know your techniques so well that you don't need to think about them.

Know your internal so well that you don't need to think about it.

Know *chi* so well that you don't need to think about it. If you have technique you can be beaten.

If you have internal you can be beaten. If you have *chi* you can be beaten. Be Empty. Be only your mind.

Know emptiness and space so well that you can move through it with your mind.

Anything else you have can be defeated, but only you know your mind.

INTERNAL QUALITY IN FIGHT SPORT

If all of this stuff is so awesome, how come you never see it used in fight sport like boxing or MMA?

Well, you do. It's just that most people don't understand what they are looking at or for. So let's do a little analysis of some of my favorite fight sport athletes and see how they stack up.

Let's stick mostly with boxing because I like it. To be honest, I don't know MMA fighters as well. But perhaps you can start looking at the qualities we're talking about and making your own assessments.

Also, these are my ideas on quality. Think for yourself and see if you agree or not and if not what qualities do you think each of these fighters has?

As you study athletes, fighters, singers, painters, or anybody else look for: *jing, chi*, and *shen*. Look for body sponsorship, *zhong ding jing*, pure internal, gravity, and *shi*.

I think you'll be surprised who seems to have what. You'll find all kinds of interesting combinations.

EXAMPLE A: MOHAMED ALI

Often called "The Greatest," probably because he was.

Excellent body sponsorship, *fa song* (melting), *chi* goes through (example: the rope-a-dope), and *zhong ding jing* (central equilibrium force). He also had excellent *shi* (playing empty space). All of these things made him fast, light, accurate, and powerful. Plus he could take a hit.

Watch him use the rope-a-dope strategy. He was laying on the ropes letting the force of the punches go through him into the rope.

Watch any number of videos on Youtube and you'll see all kinds of amazing usage of body quality and internal tactics from this guy.

Photo from Wikipedia by Ira Rosenberg. Between you and me, he may have been the first black man my mother ever saw, having grown up in a small town in Kentucky. She saw him at a gas station one day. Her only comment, with a smile on her face is, "Now that was one handsome man."

EXAMPLE B: MIKE TYSON

Iron Mike Tyson was fast, explosive, and ferocious. He was actually a fighter with a lot of high-level qualities. He had excellent body sponsorship, internal power, and gravity. You can see the opening and closing power as he moves as well as the internal going before the external and before the technique.

I don't think he could've beaten Ali, though, because he wasn't as good at playing emptiness and moving on the fly. His combinations were always very specific and trained in whereas Ali was freer in his ability to make snap decisions.

Photo from Wikipedia by Brian Birzer

EXAMPLE C: ROCKY MARCIANO

Amazing power. He had pure Internal Power, Gravity, of course Body Sponsorship, and *shi*. Watch some old videos of him and you see him beating a 200 pound heavy bag. Most are 70 pounds.

Interestingly, the internal opening and closing Marciano used was to hit on the downward stroke with almost a hammerfist to the head.

Thank you Wikipedia

Tyson had similar internal opening and closing but because he was shorter than all of his opponents he would hit with an uppercut while opening. Same power, they just hit at opposite times with it.

I could go on and on, but I hope you get the idea. As you look at fighters or other athletes, look to see what qualities they are using.

Body sponsorship? All of them should have this.

Zhong ding- central equilibrium force? This looks like the entire body goes into a hit, but is melted, relaxed, and when they get hit, the power doesn't seem to stay in their body.

Pure internal power? All athletes have internal power. But pure internal is not mixed with the external (ie, shoulder). All of the power comes from the waist, butt, and core.

Gravity power? Does the person seem to be relaxed but heavy to the opponent? Does it feel like they are filling in the space between themselves and the opponent with their energy?

Shi? Do they seem effortless while the opponent is working hard to fail? Think about Ali. He was always empty while the other guy was working hard to hit nothing. Ali was playing the emptiness in his opponent while using his maximum force to attack.

What about Barry Sanders, running back for the Lions back in the day. Empty force, pure internal power, and *shi.*

Anyway, have fun with this! As you watch professional fighting or other sports or physical entertainment, you will start to notice that internal power mastery exists in many places.

SOME THOUGHTS ON TECHNIQUE

Everything to this point has been about body movement and internal power. Now let's talk a little bit about the technique part of the equation.

By technique I'm talking about kicks, punches, chops, locks, throws, patterns, sets, forms, etc. The thing you are actually doing.

Obviously, your technique must be flawless. Your technique is one layer of what you are doing, and it has to be excellent.

On top of what you are doing with your body, let's look at a few ideas on what your technique should be.

I'm not going to give you a specific list of this combination or that one, but I will use some examples to teach a concept.

Also, a word on "styles." Don't have one. A style is a case study of somebody's body of work.

Each style was designed for a specific culture, for specific needs, a specific time period, a specific person or group of people.

A style is a study of an aspect of martial arts history and culture as a whole, but don't make it your truth.

Make styles case studies. Learn to see how they interact as fighting styles but also how they interact historically. A martial arts style is a means to an end.

Some students tell me that they don't think this is necessary, but think about it.

You must understand the why of a martial arts method to understand the martial arts method.

The why is always found in history-- it is the only way to get a glimpse of the mind of the creator of the style.

This will also help you figure out your why. You have one. You just might not know what it is yet.

Also, your why changes over time as you change.

Here are three ideas on choreographing techniques.

1. **Transition between types of technique.**
2. **Use Sentence Structure.**
3. **Flow Drills**
4. **Finding the Hole.**

Three of these four ideas are directly from TAI Martial Arts. TAI is an acronym for Transitional Action, Incorporated. The idea is to look for the transition points between different styles of martial art during a given action and incorporate them together. It was also the name of a company.

TAI was founded by a fellow named David German, who was a student of the founder of Kenpo Karate, Ed Parker. He was also a student of Al Thomas's Jujitsu. He was also a student of Leonard Lum's kung Fu.

He then started to blend these arts together.

Of course, in the 1960's and 1970's this was blasphemous. In fact there is an article in Black Belt Magazine Calling him "The Kung Fu Heretic." Now a lot of people are blending arts-- not so back then.

In the southeastern US, German teamed up with a guy named Virgil Kimmey, who trained all over Asia in the military, at one point in time he trained Frog Men, and was otherwise a pretty tough dude. Most martial artists in the South Carolina/ Georgia area can trace some lineage back to Virgil Kimmey.

I studied under a dude named Andy Watford, who is a 10th degree Black Belt under both Kimmey and German.

Unfortunately, there is a lot of politics in the TAI organization-- so I don't really associate with them too much as I just don't care about their squabbles.

Here is an article I wrote for a publication called "The New Life Journal" sometime around 2007ish I think.

About Transitional Martial Arts

Transitional Action Inc. (TAI) was the name of the system of martial arts taught by David German, my teacher until his passing in 2006.

It is all about finding the transition points between different kinds of Martial Art- focusing on kickboxing, kenpo karate, jujitsu, and Shoalin Kung Fu. He was doing MMA 30 years before it was cool.

By Derek Croley

The TAI systems of martial arts are all based upon the concept of allowing for personal freedom in application. The stated idea is to draw from several different styles of Martial Art to blend in a fashion that is appropriate to fit any given situation. Thereby giving the practitioner complete freedom of technique.

With this said, there are a few underlying principles to help you get started on working towards this freedom.

The first step is to have a base style in which you are proficient. You have to have a foundation in something. This is a lot like a good jazz musician. The best ones are very well versed in classical music, thereby allowing them to deviate from it. At my school our base is TAI-Kenpo, but it really doesn't matter what your base style is- just that you have one and know it well.

Once you have a good foundation, the next thing to do is start to look at the techniques as they are classically taught with the idea of finding out what the style is good at and what it does not address. You will find that to do this you will have to start looking at the techniques of other styles of Martial Art. There are two common errors with this step.

First, don't be so arrogant as to think that you are already doing the ultimate art. All of them have things that they specialize in.

Second, don't make the mistake of only looking for applications within your art. This won't work because, for example, an art that is really good at

*kicking generally will not be so good at take downs.
To train for take downs you would have to observe
and if you can study with somebody who is good at
the timing of take downs. The kicking guys- though
they may see and understand the technique- won't
have the timing down so the defenses that they train
will be off simply due to timing.*

*The way to address this is to cross train when you
can, watch videos of other arts, and attend seminars.
Do this with two things in mind.*

*First, how would your art deal with a particular
attack and second, how would you benefit from
stealing a technique or concept from another style in
an area that your base art isn't so strong.*

*Next, you have to look at where the spots are that you
can blend from one art to the next. In TAI we call
these transition points. The best way to begin with
this is to use two general concepts. First, use the
concept of sentence structure from Kenpo. This
means that your base technique is the noun,
something in front of it is a prefix, after the noun is a
suffix, and you can also add in a general array of ifs,
ands, withs, etc. Look for how you can take your
initial technique and then add things into it. The
second thing to consider with this concept is the
pattern, beat, or rhythm of the technique. In TAI we*

call these codes. Once you have figured out the sentence and the code for your base technique (noun) you can start to add on other stuff.

A good TAI technique should include five things: a defensive movement, and offensive movement, a lock, a takedown, and then a finish. Try to use five different arts within this sequence while using sentence structure and coding.

Finally, let's look at how to smooth over the transition. What makes a technique a TAI technique is that this blending takes place seamlessly, meaning that the average viewer would not know that you are blending arts.

To do this you have to position yourself so that the next technique is already set up, without altering the initial technique. To do this you have to plan a few steps ahead in your choreography. Let's say that you have checked a punch with your left hand to counter punch with your right hand. What if your left hand just didn't let go of the check, thereby setting up a transition into a wrist lock? The next step is to do the check, wrist lock, and punch all at the same time. This is TAI.

This is the beginning of how to choreograph techniques. By going through this process you will soon discover that it no longer matters which arts you say you are using. This study will allow you to achieve complete technical freedom as it teaches you how to break away from pre-choreographed routines.

Anyway, let's look into these in a little bit more detail.

TRANSITION BETWEEN TYPES OF TECHNIQUES.

This is the idea of finding the places where one art ends and another begins.

Can you take a striking art and find where to put the locks?

Can you take a throwing art and find where to put the kicks?

Where are the transitions?

This is an exercise in creativity as well as practicality. You need to be able to take advantage of whatever opportunity is available to you and, with a flexible mind, take advantage.

David German would use a product called the Kenpoman to teach the beginning of this idea. It is a striking dummy with a rotation arm that is used to teach the idea of rhythm and timing. I've also never seen anything that will improve your hand speed like it. Well, I am a big fan of speed bags.

Anyway, the Kenpoman method develops what David would call Codes. These are the natural rhythms that develop from the use of the dummy.

He would then take these Codes, clap them to teach them, and use them to create techniques. Then he would have you stick different techniques into the code with the same rhythm.

This exercise was an excellent way to creatively play with different choreography of technique. With the Codes you are able to really figure out where the transition points are and what you can transition to.

USE SENTENCE STRUCTURE

This is a concept from Kenpo Karate. The idea is to assemble a technique like a sentence.

Your primary technique is your noun. Say it's block, chop, punch.

A prefix is something you add to the front. What if you kick the bad buy in the shin and then block, chop, punch.

A suffix goes after the noun. Maybe a reaping throw?

An "And" would be when you stack another technique while you are doing the first one. Maybe you block and lock the wrist while you chop, then you kick the groin as you punch.

We can also think about If/Then statements.

This is the idea of following the response of your opponent. IF he does then then I do this.

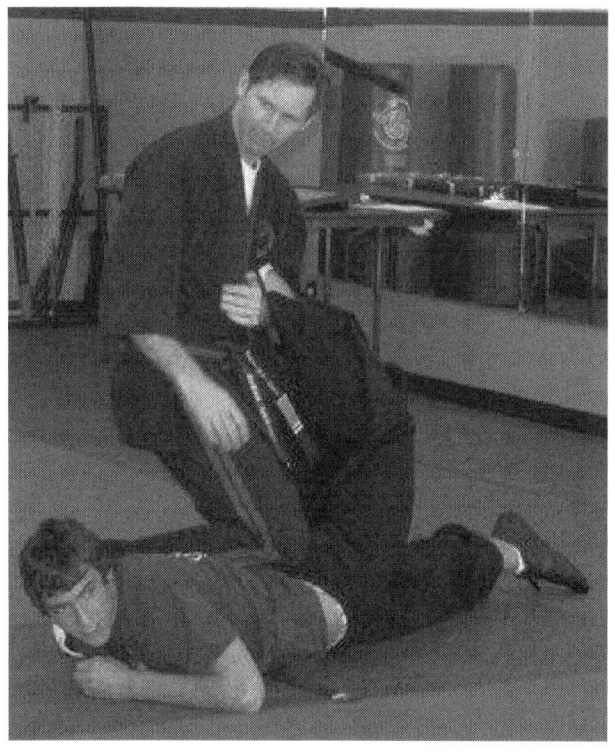

An example would be in grappling. From the guard position, I try a sweep. If I can't, then I return down to a kimura lock. If that doesn't work, I try a triangle choke. If that doesn't work, I try an armbar. If that doesn't work, I try another lock from the list above in any order.

If your opponent does this, then you do that.

An important point. Know the laws on self-defense where you live.

With that said, let's go over some things to consider as you build your martial art.

Here are a few things that I personally think a martial arts method should have.

You can take this idea and run with it. It makes things a lot of fun. But remember, don't limit yourself to any particular genre of martial arts. Mix any techniques and ideas you want.

FLOW DRILLS

This is a concept that I learned form Brian Adams with his Integrated Martial Arts System. It combines old school Kenpo, Traditional Jujitsu, Modern Arnis, and White Tiger Kung Fu. He tends to use the escrima stick fighting as his foundation for movement and has some really great ideas on how to assemble technique.

One of them is the extensive use of flow drills. This is where, with no choreography, one person attacks. Then the other defends and counters, then the first person defends and counters. Back and forth. Every time you move your feet to put yourself in a superior position. It's a lot like sparring where you are taking turns and finding where to move.

In fact, that is sort of the point of the exercise-- finding where to move.

Take that, Villain!

This drill allows you to figure out where to put your body, where attacks are likely to come from, and how to move fluidly from one thing to the next.

You of course then do this drill with sticks and knives and whatever other variables you can think of to add in. You can use all striking, all kicking, all locking, mixing it up in any way you see fit.

It's a fun drill to build fluidity of technique.

FINDING THE HOLE

This is another George Xu concept. His idea of technique is to not have one. As he says, a tiger doesn't have a "tiger technique." Finding the hole is the notion that you read where your opponent doesn't have anything and you attack that.

Move like a beaver through the water around their defenses and changing position.

Move like a dragon through the clouds, keeping your true power hidden while the rest of you stays invisible to your opponent.

Basically, hide your internal power and have your arm technique not be what it seems to be. Find Where your opponent is not and go there. Even as they change, you change as well to go where they are not.

Find the hole and attack it. Just like Lando blowing up the new Death Star in Return of the Jedi. Good times.

Krav Maga heightens perception and transforms fear into something more productive.

Imi Lichtenfeld

10 PRINCIPLES TO FOLLOW

My first classroom training in Israel at the Wingate Institute was an excellent day to wear a cup. The instructor was absolutely brilliant.

The first thing he did was pick somebody in the class, me of course, and punch me in the crotch demonstrating a technique.

Welcome to Krav Maga.

I was, in fact, wearing an athletic supporter. So, you know, I had that going for me.

If you don't get it, for us martial arts people this is funny. Cup checks are funny.

Don't worry about it.

Anyway, he then wrote a list on the board of the basic principles of Krav Maga. You see, Krav Maga does have some distinctive techniques, like the 360 defense, but overall it's really a body of concepts with techniques that are fluid based upon the need of the user at the time.

Of course, I could say the same thing about internal martial arts. I've spent a great deal of time discussing a series of concepts, not specific techniques.

This makes me think of a conversation that I recently had with a friend named Aaron Hensley from North Augusta, SC.

Aaron is a 7th degree black belt under Chuck Norris, and is an incredible martial artist. Aaron made the point that the very concept of style in martial art is going away.

There is so much communication available these days that it is very easy to see the flaws in any style and begin cross training to fill in the gaps. In fact, it would be foolish not to.

His view, and I agree, is that martial arts in America will be more about studying the body of work of an individual person instead of this or that style.

I completely agree.

Now, what does this have to do with these 10 principles?

Simple really, while the idea of doing a style is less relevant than it used to be, the idea of working within a series of principles becomes much more useful.

These 10 principles overlap in terms of what they are from and who my influences were.

I suspect that several of my teachers could look at these and say, yes, these are from me. Perhaps.

One of my other friends, Chris Garland is a Veteran Army Ranger. We also grew up together teaching at the same martial arts school in Aiken, SC while we were both in high school.

One of his ideas that I like a lot is that when you are looking at different kinds of martial art don't look for what that style does that is unique, look at what all of the different styles agree on.

Because what they agree on is the stuff that actually has the highest success rate.

Well, with all of that said, here are the 10 things that should be considered in all martial arts scenarios.

Remember how we started this book talking about art vs sport vs real world application?

These concepts, in my opinion should apply to all of them.

1. Safety
2. Simultaneous Offense and Defense
3. Flinch Response
4. Be Explosive and Fast
5. Get off of the X

6. The 4 Parts of a Technique
7. The Timeline of Attack
8. The Force Continuum
9. Environmental Awareness
10. Be Deceptive

Let's go through each of these in more detail.

As you read these, please remember that I am not an attorney and am in no way offering legal advice, only my opinions.

1. SAFETY

This is pretty simple. If you get hurt, you can't train.

If you hurt your partner, they won't train with you.

Advanced practitioners of any type of fighting, grappling or striking, often don't like sparring with beginners because beginners don't understand safety well enough.

If you are working with somebody in a training format or a professional one, your safety and theirs is your personal responsibility.

Take it seriously.

Consider this is the type of training that you do. Remember, fitness is important.

However, do not break your body in the name of fitness. That is the opposite of fitness.

The statement "no pain no gain" is simply wrong. I'm not suggesting that you shouldn't work hard-- of course you should. But you need to work smart.

Challenge yourself, push yourself, but don't break yourself.

2. SIMULTANEOUS OFFENSE AND DEFENSE

Most martial arts that I know of follow this idea. Some practitioners don't, but that's neither here nor there.

The basic idea is to make sure you are blocking and hitting at the same time.

The reason for this is timing.

If somebody is trying to hit you once, then it is highly likely that they will do it again. You need to stop the attacker's momentum and disrupt their intent.

To do this, you can never just block; you have to attack as well.

This means block and punch at the same time, or block and kick, or whatever, but make sure you are hitting the bad guy.

This is especially important in knife defenses. The best defense I have ever seen for a knife is to punch the bad guy in the face as hard as you can and run for it.

My friend Terry Shea. Vietnam Vet, 8th Degree Black Belt, Iron Palm Master, and all around great guy who is really interesting to talk to.

Of course block as well to minimize how much you get stabbed.

My Krav Maga instructor, Ernie Kirk, likes to use stress drills to teach this point.

He refers to it with a smile as "experiential learning." A stress drill is where you have somebody actually attack you with a practice knife.

I mean actually attack you. There is no asking for permission, no "wait, wait, let me try that again," a real attack.

Then you do your best to not "die."

The thing is, of course you "die" in the drill.

But you discover pretty quick what is actually going to work and what is not.

Obviously, knife attacks are extremely dangerous and there is no "good" defense, mostly because of the psychology of the attacker.

They are highly aggressive and have a strong intent to kill. Hard to defend against that.

With that said, it is best to do your best anyway.

And the best way to defend against a knife is to always assume there is one and always use simultaneous offence and defense.

3. FLINCH RESPONSE

Performing simultaneous attack and defend is a trained response. It is useful when you have some forewarning and are able to do it.

But sometimes you don't have forewarning. Something happens, like an unforeseen punch, and you instinctively bring your hands up.

Or maybe something is about to hit you in the groin and you instinctively cross your legs.

Here's the trick.

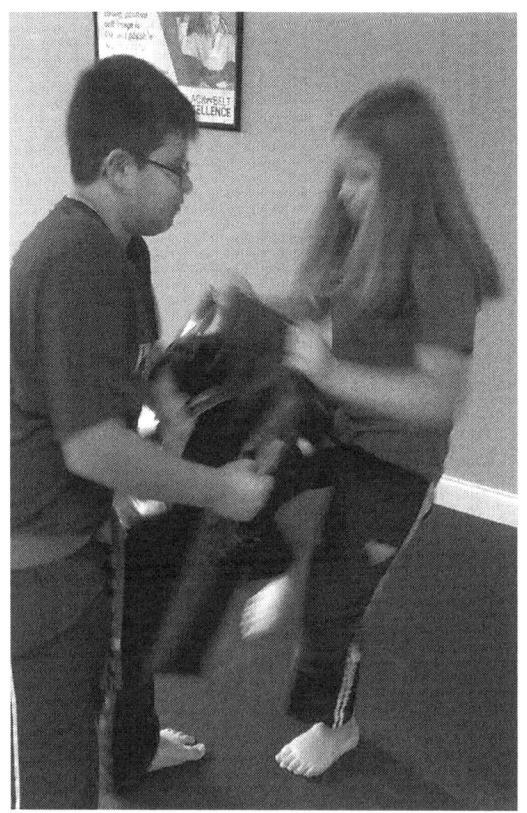

Don't try to train out your natural flinch response to potential injury.

Just add your punches, kicks or other attacks to the end of your flinch response.

Wingate Instructor Alain Cohen has an excellent video on youtube.com about the differences and uses of Simultaneous movement vs flinch Response. It's called "[KRAV MAGA IS NOT TRUE]."

I personally think he has the best Krav Maga video series on Youtube.

4. BE EXPLOSIVE AND FAST

This is a common theme amongst all of my teachers. Be explosive and be fast. Also, be relaxed and empty. As the old saying goes, "slow is smooth, and smooth is fast." Be fast.

The reason is simple. Force=Mass x Acceleration.

You have as much mass you as have, it's not going to change over the course of the fight.

So first you must have good Body Sponsorship (footwork, rotational force from the hips, and transfer of weight from the feet), then you have to move explosively and as fast as you can to have maximum acceleration.

Mike Tyson in his prime was just about the perfect fighter.

The trick is to be relaxed before, during, and after the movement. As we discussed in great detail earlier, relaxing means that you only use the correct muscles to move and don't have the wrong ones fighting you and decreasing your power.

Being explosive and fast means that you will be able to hit harder, hit more often, and return to a superior defensive position sooner.

https://www.youtube.com/watch?v=5XqpEjVrDEo

Bill Wallace mentions that he never tried to hit anybody hard, he just tried to be as fast as possible.

With this approach he didn't get tired in his professional fights, and he still had 10 knockouts out of 23 fights.

Not bad. Not bad at all.

5. GET OFF OF THE X

This is a term I learned from Ernie Kirk, and I quite like it.

Did you ever watch the Roadrunner and Wile E. Coyote cartoons?

Wile E. would often draw an X on the ground where he planned on his bomb hitting the Roadrunner.

We would like for your personal bad guy to be as successful at hitting you as Wile E. Coyote is.

Much like the Roadrunner, never stay on the X.

If you somebody wants to hit you do not stay where they plan on you being.

Even in the middle of an attack, try to not be where you are supposed to be. I also submit that you should obtain a position of offensive or defensive superiority.

6. THE 4 PARTS OF A TECHNIQUE

In any technique, I teach that there are 4 things that need to happen.

This again, is from Ernie Kirk.

1. **Identify the threat.**
2. **Stop the immediate threat.**
3. **Stop the secondary threat.**
4. **Escape.**

Let's break this down a little bit.

First, in order to defend against a bad guy, you have to recognize that there is a bad guy.

You can't stop an attack you don't know is coming. So pay attention.

Next, when you are being attacked, the first thing to deal with is the first problem.

Just like in the "Seven Habits of Highly Successful People," *"First things first."* Stop the first attack first, then worry about whatever is next.

Speaking of which, after you stop the first attack, then do something to stop the next one. This generally comes in the form of hitting the bad guy really hard in the face, but that is variable.

But remember, if a first attack came, a second will be on the way unless you stop it.

And last, you need to escape. If you find yourself in a physical conflict, ie a fight, you have probably walked into some kind of a trap.

This is a trap where you don't know the variables, details, nor even the players involved. Therefore, it's best to escape as soon as possible.

Remember, there is no scoreboard. In self defense surviving is winning.

7. THE TIMELINE OF AN ATTACK

For my entire martial arts education, from the age of 8 on, the teacher would often if not always say something that I often find myself saying.

"You can never hit anybody ever. Now let's practice punches."

This does not make sense.

...ladies and gentlemen of this supposed jury, I have one final thing I want you to consider. Ladies and gentlemen, this is Chewbacca. Chewbacca is a Wookiee from the planet Kashyyyk. But Chewbacca lives on the planet Endor. Now think about it; that does not make sense! **South Park's Chewbacca Defense**

In fact, the Chewbacca Defense is the Karate Kid Crane Kick of the legal world. No can defense.

"I will totally crane kick you."

The thing is, you are supposed to defend yourself when you have to, but not hit anybody when you don't need to.

So how do you communicate this to a student?

How do you stress test this so it's more than just a lecture?

Well, enter going to the Wingate Institute in Israel. One of the stress drills that we did was called a Timeline.

The concept is to identify where in the attack process is the bad guy and what is your best response at that time.

In many cases, this boils down to the range at which you identify the problem.

It goes like this:

1. **Long-range: Run away.**
   You identify the bad guy while there is still enough space between you to leave. You should leave.

2. **Mid-range: Kick and run.**
   The bad guy is too close to run from, but too far to engage. If you run at kicking range you get

caught, so kick the bad guy-- generally in the groin- and then run.

3. **Mid-range with a weapon Presented: Smack the weapon, kick, and run.**
   The bad guy is at mid range, but has presented a weapon. However, he hasn't started his attack with it yet-- he's holding it in front of himself. Smack the hand the weapon is in. Smack it really, really hard. Then kick him in the groin, and then run.

4. **Close Range: Do a technique and run.**
   The bad guy is close enough for you to do a technique, then do one and run.

Did you notice the theme of each level is to escape?

Remember, your objective is to survive.

There are too many unknowns in a violent situation, too many things that can go wrong.

Now to do the drill, have the person who is our good guy close their eyes.

At my school we refer to the person doing the drill as the "Space Monkey."

The Space Monkey closes their eyes. The evil bad guy goes to one of the ranges in question.

When the instructor yells "open your eyes," the Space Monkey does the appropriate response.

This trains quick decision making under stress. Sometimes we'll have the Space Monkey do burpees, spin in circles, or whatever we can think of to get the heart rate up before they open their eyes.

Sometimes the Space Monkey gets stabbed by a foam knife with no verbal warning, or hit with a body shield with no warning, just to add some more stress.

As the student gets better, you can also have them defend against things that are not on the list.

It's good if there are surprise elements that they don't know yet, occasionally. All to build quick decision making skills.

Be safe, but creative with these drills. They are great!

8. THE FORCE CONTINUUM

This is a way to think about what level of force is appropriate for any different situation. There are a few components to this.

Remember that the primary objective of self-defense against violence is to escape. Your objective is not to be Batman, it is to do what you must to facilitate your escape by creating escape routes and opportunities.

You do not want to stay in a violent situation as you almost never know what variables are at play.

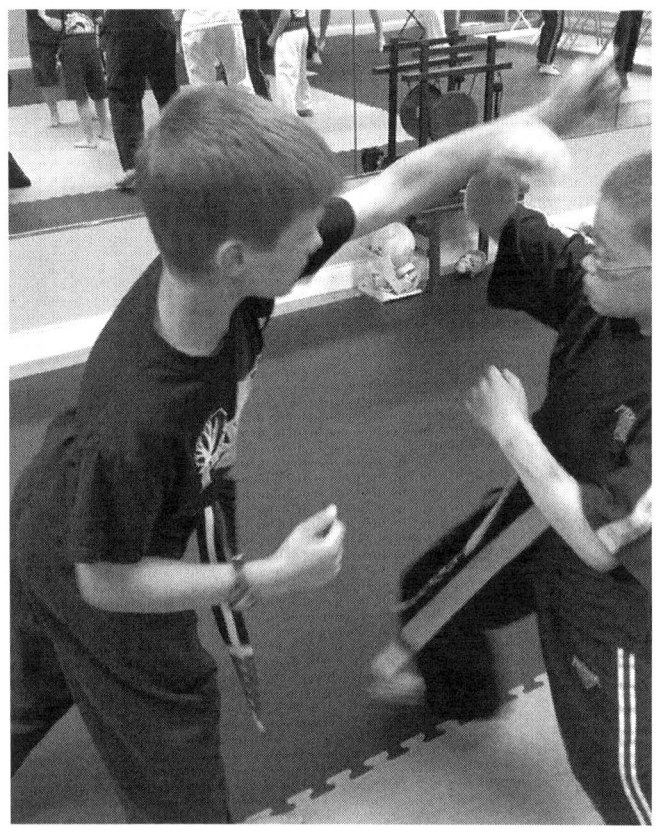

First, use an appropriate and necessary level of force to avoid getting hurt with the objective of escape.

You wouldn't hit somebody for calling you a bad name-- that's too much force.

At the same time, you need to defend yourself against somebody who means you serious bodily harm. Try to use appropriate force for the situation. Also, consider who the other person is and only use the amount of force needed to avoid getting hurt.

We would vastly prefer to use no force at all and find other solutions to our problems.

Second, learn to read the body language of violence.

You should read "The Gift of Fear," by Gavin De Becker.

My best advice is to become a student of body language.

What does it mean when somebody bows out their chest and turns red?

What does it mean when somebody reaches behind their back with their shoulders pointed towards you?

What does it mean when in the middle of a heated conversation somebody turns their right shoulder away from you and begins to turn away from you?

What does it mean when somebody has on an unseasonably large coat and is looking around nervously or perhaps is walking with great focus?

You guessed it, all of these things mean that things might be about to get real. Whatever you do, you need to be able to…...

Third, be able to articulate what you saw the bad guy do and why you did whatever you did.

Become a student of self-defense enough that you can justify your actions to either a jury, a judge, an employer, a teacher, a parent, or whoever else you need to justify yourself too.

Some books to consider are anything by Rory Miller, perhaps "Facing Violence" would be a good start.

Then maybe "The Little Black Book of Violence," by Kane and Wilder. From there you can read all kinds of stuff.

My book is not enough in this regard, there are a few books by some very knowledgeable people that are excellent resources for you.

Don't speculate-- educate yourself.

Fourth, violence has consequence.

You are not Batman. Situations get really bad in unexpected ways very quickly.

"The Little Black Book of Violence" is an excellent discussion of this. I strongly recommend that you read it.

If at all possible, avoid violent confrontation. One of my teachers used to say,

"If you get into a fight with somebody, and they break both of your arms-- but you break both of their arms and both of their legs-- who won the fight?"

Kids will say that you did. But of course, the answer is,

"The doctor won the fight-- he's making money off of this. Neither of you can work or even go to the bathroom by yourself.

You didn't win anything, and now you can't feed your family."

A fine point if you ask me.

Fifth, disparity of force.

This is the concept that you and the person you are defending yourself against are not equal in terms of your potential and ability for violence.

In the eighties there was a thing going around that as a black belt you had to register yourself with the law since you are now a lethal weapon. Oh yeah, sure.

This is clearly not true and is a lesson taught by the deranged. Or maybe it's like a snipe hunt or a Kessel Run. I'm not sure, but either way it's not true.

What I'm talking about is what if a 105 pound woman is attacked by a 250 pound man?

What if there are 5 bad guys with knives and bats and you have, well, your fists?

This is the kind of disparity of force I'm talking about.

How do you think this might change a self-defense situation?

Of course, as always, avoiding violent confrontation and escaping is always our objective.

One time when Brook (my wife) and I lived in China we were in the back of a city bus going home. We were trying to decide if we wanted to stay in China for another year, or if we wanted to just go back to the States.

As we got off of the bus, a guy came running across the street about 50 feet from us. Five or six guys were chasing him and they all had 2x4's. They caught up to him on our side of the street and began to beat him to death. This was just after lunch.

Brook said to me, "Go do something!"

But there was nothing I could do except get killed as well. There were five or six armed people.

The disparity of force was too high. So we left. We would have called the police, but they were already there watching just like we were.

We learned two things that day. First, we decided not to stay in China, and second, even though I didn't have the fancy phrase for it, I learned about disparity of force.

There are two sides to disparity. First, don't enter a fight you can't win. And second, weapons can be equalizers.

If in a fight between two 150-pound men one of them pulls a gun and shoots the other, he is going to get into legal trouble.

But what if a 12-year-old girl shoots a grown man who picks a fight with her? Not the same, is it.

Don't start nothin' won't be nothin', Jered.

9. ENVIRONMENTAL AWARENESS

Don't get hit by a bus.

This is something of a dark joke. There is a story of a man who defends himself successfully against bad guys and in his retreat is hit by a bus.

The lesson of course is to always pay attention to your environment.

Here are a few things to consider in a self-defense situation.

Take note of your geography.

Think about things to fall off of, walls, doors, unstable terrain...Where are you and what's it like?

In training consider adding variability to the terrain.

It is very easy to trip over things, run into things and not see things when you are under stress in a self-defense situation.

Train for this. Train for avoiding things and keeping your balance, but also train for recovering from a fall. It'll happen.

Look for other attackers.

Predators often hunt in packs. The person in front of you is often not the only bad guy. Keep your head on the swivel.

I've heard of different formations, often in teams of three-- though not necessarily.

One person stops in front of you while the other two block visibility for witnesses from the side.

One person walks next to you, hook punches you in the face, two others drag you into an ally.

Stuff like that. Like I said, keep your head on the swivel.

Look for Friends

Are there people around who can help you if they can hear you yelling, otherwise get their attention, or you can get to them?

Bad guys don't want to get caught-- they want to stay being bad guys.

Over the years I've heard different pieces of advice about what to yell. I've never seen any actual data on what is the most effective things to say.

I do think that the most valuable thing you can do is make a big fuss and make yourself known. So be loud, be difficult to manage and don't stop.

Opportunities

What opportunities for escape or attack exist for you? What can you see? Think like Captain Kirk and remember, there is always a way! If you are still awake you are still in the fight!

Weapons

What weapons do you have or are available to you?

Can you pick up a rock, or a bottle?

Can you hit the bad guy with your cell phone or a book?

Did you bring a knife or a gun?

Whether it's a weapon of opportunity or a planned defensive system think about what you have available to you.

A word of advice in guns and knives. There is a saying, "Owning a spatula doesn't make you a chef."

The meaning is that owning and carrying a gun doesn't mean that you know how to use it.

Train yourself and educate yourself if you choose to carry a weapon.

People to protect.

Do you have a child or a spouse with you, or somebody else you need to protect? Think about how you might do that.

We offer something called "Third Party Protection Training." This involves tactics to protect somebody from a bad guy.

It can be simple things like don't redirect weapons towards who you're with. Try to create space for whoever you're with away from the bad guy. Stuff like that.

The basic idea is simple. Protect the people you are with via body position, direction of weapons, and this could also affect how much force you use.

If I think a bad guy is going to hurt my kids, you bet I'll use more force.

Consider visibility.

The news like to say things like, "The bad guy attacked unarmed and in broad daylight." As if these are actually relevant factors to a bad guy choosing to do bad guy stuff.

A person can have the ability to kill and the intent to do so regardless of if they are armed or not.

Also, the presence or absence of light is not even remotely a relevant factor.

With that said, the amount of light can be a relevant factor for you. Is it light or dark?

Can you identify the bad guy later?

Can you see weapons right now?

Can you read body language?

Can witnesses see what is going on?

Try to avoid putting yourself in a situation where you will have poor visibility.

Around here the mall gets crazy busy around Christmas.

It is not uncommon to park in the day and it's night by the time you get back out to your car.

With this knowledge in mind it makes sense to park close to a light in the parking lot, just in case.

Also, if you get the feeling that something is off, stores will send somebody to your car with you upon request.

Witnesses.

Are there people who saw what happened? This can help you later. What did they see?

At what point in time did the cell phones come out and how does the video look?

Did you get punched in the face and then beat up the bad guy-- but all they got on video was you beating somebody up?

I know a guy who was manipulated by a girl to go to a bar. She then picked a fight with a different fellow.

The guy I know didn't know that his date had started the fight (she was slick like that) and when the other guy pushed her, he stepped in to defend her, there were words exchanged, and he ended up beating up the other guy.

Of course the surveillance video looks totally different. It looks like he and the girl just attacked the other dude. So things didn't go so well legally for the fellow I know.

These are things to consider before you get into a fight. I suggest that you try to avoid getting into a fight in the first place.

Escape Routes.

Always be on the lookout for ways to escape.

Think about this even when you are just going out in public. What if an active shooter shows up? What if there is a fire? You need to know how to get out of wherever you are.

During the violent situation or anywhere in the timeline it is relevant to know how you are going to leave. Have this pre planned.

Don't get taken.

And last, don't get taken away.

Remember that there are two crime scenes in an abduction scenario Crime Scene 1 is the location of the abduction, and Crime Scene 2 is the secluded location where the real bad stuff happens.

Fight with everything you have to avoid going to crime scene 2.

Remember, *if you are still awake, you are still in the fight.*

10. BE DECEPTIVE

This covers a few different things. First, it can be to your advantage to act weaker and less prepared during a self-defense situation.

For example, if somebody points a gun at you, could you cower and beg and talk about your kids right before you attack?

It seems that it is best to pounce between statements. Your voice will change if you move quickly while you are talking, and you might give away the jig.

Maybe you would benefit from acting more confident or even violent when facing violence.

One lady at a self-defense workshop told me that she caused an attacker to leave by picking up a rock and yelling at him while using what she referred to as her "crazy eyes."

Often times, simply carrying yourself more confidently than you may feel prevents a lot of unwanted advances.

Whatever the case, it is often best to not show your cards too soon.

This is very situational; you'll have to decide how to do this and what the best tactics will be at the time.

Being deceptive is also useful during the actual fight. This could apply to sport fighting or self-defense.

First, Disguise the Technique.

Bill "Superfoot" Wallace went 23-0 in professional kickboxing largely with the idea that he was going to kick you. It was going to be a side kick, round kick, or hook kick with his left leg. The thing is nobody knew which kick it was going to be.

He would chamber his knee in the same place no matter what kick he was going to throw, so you couldn't see it until too late.

He also might be tricky and throw a few kicks for you to block, chamber his knee and when you instinctively go to block it he would kick somewhere else.

He would also always use the same, footwork regardless of what technique he was going to do-- punch or kick.

If it always looks the same it's hard to tell what is going to happen next.

In a different context, could you do something as simple as hold your hands in front of you in a "don't hit me" position?

This is the same as having your guard up, right? Could you hit the bad guy from a "don't hit me" position? Sure.

Second, Disguise the Distance.

It would be nice if there was a way to make it so the bad guy or your opponent didn't think you could hit them from your current range, but you actually can.

Oh wait, there is a way to do that. Again, from the Superfoot system.

1. Lead stepping.
   Use your front foot to cover the ground with your back foot following. This beats other methods where your first move doesn't cover ground. This gets you there fast and your first

move doesn't give you away. Remember, use the same lead step for punching or kicking.

2. Jumping jacks.
   If you bring both of your feet under yourself like doing a jumping jack (just don't do the arms) your base foot is set to kick. This works really well as you have covered ground to kick, but your torso didn't move so it doesn't look like it. Play with this, it's pretty cool.

3. Angular stepping.
   What if you lead step, but them step to a progressive angle with your back foot? you get a similar effect as with the jumping jack step, just off to the side. You don't look like you can hit the bad guy , but you can because you didn't step flat sideways with your back foot, there was forward progress.

As you can see, you use your footwork to disguise your distance.

Can you do this in a self defense situation? Of course. You can apply good footwork to any situation.

Third, Disguise the Timing.

It's also nice when the other person doesn't know when you are going to hit them.

In sparring, the Superfoot system teaches that your opponent knows you are eventually going to hit them.

So create a footwork pattern, like a bouncing 4 count for example, and learn to throw any of your techniques from anywhere in the 4 count.

Then in your mind make it a song. Change where you hit in the song count.

In self-defense tactics, attack when you aren't supposed to. Attack when you are not expected and in a way that is unexpected.

You can use footwork, your words, your facial expression and body language, or even your aggressiveness.

Bad guys become very surprised when you become very violent very quickly. So that is a possibility.

You'll have to assess this at the time and do the best you can.

The general idea is of course to be as deceptive as possible to keep your opponent off balance. mentally and physically.

There is a story of Miyamoto Musashi, widely regarded as the greatest Japanese swordsman.

I think he was a wandering psychopath as he went around challenging people to fights and then killing them "for honor." I don't see much honor in that.

However, among martial artists, my opinion is not at all popular about the man. Anyway, he was very good at what he did.

One story is that he challenged a fellow named **Sasaki Kojiro** to a fight, and to make a long story short, Musashi was hours late.

Sasaki was so mad and put out by the disrespect of the tardiness that he lost the fight.

Musashi used deception and off-balancing his opponent to win. Get the whole story here:

http://www.musashi-miyamoto.com/sasaki-kojiro.html

Though I don't like what he did, I completely respect his genius in how he did it. Constantly thinking outside of the box to keep his opponents off balance.

IN SUMMARY

In summary, begin with the end in mind. Figure out why you are doing martial arts. Is it for the art, the sport, the defense? All are great and you are not limited to one thing.

Learn the difference between *jing, chi*, and *shen*. Build your skill of *ting jing*- or how to touch people and "listen" to what they are doing with their bodies.

To build power and longevity in your mind and body, learn internal martial art and apply the concepts to any art or arts you want.

Master the 5 aspects of internal martial arts.

1. Body Sponsorship.
2. *Zhong Ding.*
3. Pure Internal.
4. Gravity.
5. Space Power and *Shi.*

Master the techniques of whatever art you do, but keep an open mind and be willing to change based upon what seems to work for you.

Become a student of self-defense concepts. Read books on the subject. Do safe but realistic stress tests. Think about the 10 points presented in this book.

1. Safety
2. Simultaneous Offense and Defense
3. Flinch Response
4. Be Explosive and Fast
5. Get off of the X
6. The 4 Parts of a Technique
7. The Timeline of Attack
8. The Force Continuum
9. Environmental Awareness
10. Be Deceptive

If you do these things, continue to train, continue to think, continue to persevere you will become extraordinary.

Remember this sequence of learning. 1. Learn new material. 2. Practice that material. 3. Stress test.

Don't practice until you get it right, practice until you can't get it wrong.

And last but not least, remember that *Mastery is a mindset, not a destination.* The people who inspire me are those who never stop learning, never stop training, and never stop improving.

Enjoy your journey, take your vision quest, and push the envelope of what is possible.

FINAL THOUGHT: RESPECTFUL IRREVERENCE

Kill the Buddha.

All too often we put our teachers on pedestals. It is important to remember that all of these people are still people.

"Kill the Buddha" means whatever you think the Buddha is, whatever you think the truth is, or the path, or the way....Whatever you think it is, you are not finished. Your view is incomplete.

I'm not saying to disrespect your teachers. Of course not. I'm saying to remember that they are human and subject to the human condition. We are all flawed.

But this is a good thing! First, this means that whatever knowledge and skill your teacher has obtained was through hard work, training, and experience.

You can do that as well.

Second, your teacher has certain thought patterns, perspectives, and experiences that have shaped what they think and do. Everybody sees things in certain ways.

Remember this as you train. Your teacher presents things from a certain point of view. The trick is that you should first learn the full teaching, then you can look at the perspective and make adjustments for yourself.

And third, we all have flaws. So does your teacher. As you learn an art, try not to absorb the personal flaws of your teacher.

Learn to think for yourself. Remember, every martial art is a case study of one person's body of work.

There is really no such thing as a "traditional" martial art as we all change things a little. It is unavoidable. It is also desirable.

Test things. Try things. Experiment. Figure out what works for you and what doesn't. Allow your education to be a process and enjoy that process.

BONUS MATERIAL: 24 SECRETS OF XU GUO MING

1. Wu Wei (no effort) defeat You Wei (have effort). No Fist defeat have Fist. No Root defeat have Root. No technique defeat technique.

2. Nobody knows me, I know enemy defeat Everybody know me, I don't know my enemy.

3. Predator defeat Prey.

4. Unit force defeat partial force. Harmony defeat No Harmony.

5. Ying Yang balance defeat too much Ying or Yang.

6. Hard and Soft Harmony defeat too Hard and Soft Harmony.

7. No Root but everywhere is root defeat 3 feet root and floating root.

8. Shi has Nei Shi and Wai Shi. Have Shi defeat no Shi. Alive Shi defeat dead Shi. Big Shi defeat Small Shi. Understand Shi defeat don't understand Shi. Borrow Shi defeat being borrowed Shi.

9. Body middle section move first, Internal and external Shi arrive before hand defeat body hand together, body move, hand not harmony or hand arrive first.

10. Whole body is fist. Whole body harmony to one. Touch my body any point is touching my whole body defeat whole body is not one.

11. Open/Close, Up/Down, Sparrow/Turn, Empty/Full, Four become one defeat only one or two factors.

12. Intelligence and scientific body art defeat ox power and unscientific body movements.

13. 3-D movement plus fast slow and empty full change (5 factor) defeat 1-D and 2-D movement.

14. Internal Shi no concave convex defeat have concave convex. Internal Shi defeat solid Nei Jing.

15. Chi defeat Jing. Empty agile defeat solid and firm.

16. Body volume attack defeat point attack. Physical inside energy field defeat physical outside energy field.

17. Yi before the fist, internal and external Shi before the fist defeat Yi after the fist, fist Jing before internal and external Shi.

18. Heaven defeat earth. Body mass in the sky defeat body weight on earth.

19. Maximum body art and spirit defeat no maximum body art and spirit.

20. Forget me defeat focus me.

21. Gravity at enemy's body defeat gravity on myself.

22. Big group muscle do the work defeat small group muscle do the work.

23. Internal defeat external.

24. Lower body martial art defeat upper body martial art.

ABOUT THE AUTHOR

Who is this guy and why is he writing a book like this? Well, this is me along with a cut and paste special from my school website bio! Lazy, yes. Do I care? No.

With over 28 years of teaching experience, Derek Croley has dedicated his life to helping people get into the best shape of their lives, learn real self defense, and to have the Black Belt Excellence mindset.

Having taught thousands of students over the years, he has worked tirelessly to have a positive impact on all of them with progressive programs and teaching methods designed to maximize their abilities on and off of the mat. To this end he is constantly working to improve himself as a martial artist and educator in an effort to provide the highest quality of education available in the world, right here in Asheville.

Derek Croley began studying martial arts at the age of 8 and began teaching at the age of 13 as an assistant instructor. He received his first Black Belt at age 15 under Shihan Dave Kovar in Sacramento, California. Kovar now operates some of the largest and most successful schools in the country and is internationally known for his teaching methods.

While still 15, Derek moved to Aiken, South Carolina where he became an Instructor under Grand Master Andy Watford. Grand Master Watford is a 10th Degree Black Belt under Grand Master David German and Grand Master Virgil Kimmey.

After completing a degree in Business Management from Clemson University Derek and his wife Brook moved to Jilin City, in the Jilin Provence of Manchurian China. There, he further perfected his skills under Grand Master Liu Chan Shan. Under Grand Master Liu, he was the first Westerner ever to learn the art of Taiji Yuan Gong Chan Chuan, and is one of a few people in the world who knows this secret art. With the blessing of Po Rin Fu he is allowed to teach this art openly in America. While in Northeastern China he also earned the title of Shifu (teacher) in Liu Style Tai Chi Chuan as well as Yuan Gong Chan Chuan.

In 2005 he was awarded the title of Master Instructor in David German's US TAI Martial Arts Association.

Derek now trains and is a Master Instructor under Grand Master George (Guo Ming) Xu in the Internal Martial Arts of Xu Shen Chuan. He has been awarded an 8th degree Black Belt under Grand Master Xu.

He has written four books on the Martial Arts (including The Physical Structure of Martial Arts and How to Approach Tai Chi Like a Master), published several articles, and produced several educational videos on a wide variety of topics. His newest book is "The Six Steps to Self Mastery," and is available on Amazon.

In 2007 he was featured in a series of TAI Kenpo Instructional videos from Lotus Video Productions. He was highlighted in the silver screen documentary The Why? of Tai Chi by filmmaker Bruce Kennedy and choreographed the fights between Peter Pan and Captain Hook in the 2009 Asheville Community Theater production of Peter Pan.

In 2008 Master Croley was awarded an honorary PhD in Asian Martial Arts Philosophy from the University of Asian Martial Arts Study via the USA Martial Arts Hall of Fame. This is an honorary martial arts industry award for contribution to the arts and years of service.

He has also been greatly honored to have been appointed as a Vice President of WACIMA (Worldwide Association of Chinese Internal Martial Arts) by the International President of the organization, Grand Master Xu.

In December of 2010, Croley took several students to China once again, studying under noted Grand Masters Wu Ji in the art of Lan Shou and Shi Sen Lin in the art of Baqua.

In 2011 he earned his Black Belt in Grand Master Brian Adams "Integrated Martial Arts." Adams was an original student of Martial Arts Pioneers Ed Parker, Bruce Lee, Doo Wai, and Danny Inosonto.

2013 was his 30th year of practicing martial arts.

In 2014 Derek became a certified Krav Maga Instructor under Ernie Kirk of Krav Maga Universal.

In 2015 he was honored at the Virgil D. Kimmey Martial Arts College with a 6th Degree Black Belt in the International TAI Martial Arts Association.

In May of 2016, Derek went to the Wingate Institute in Netanya, Israel to train in Krav Maga. The Wingate Institute is the birthplace of the art, and this training camp was put on by the actual Wingate Staff.

In June of 2017 he earned his Black Belt in Bill "Superfoot" Wallace's Superfoot Kickboxing System.

Derek now resides in Asheville, North Carolina with his wife and children. He has numerous Black Belts and Instructor Certifications, he is the owner of Croley's Premier Martial Arts, President of The White Oak Martial Arts Association, Vice President of WACIMA (the Worldwide Association for Chinese Internal Martial Arts), the 2008-2009 President of the Asheville West Rotary Club, and a member of the US Martial Arts Hall of Fame.

My brother Jeff, my dog Boss (named after Boss Hog from the tv show "Dukes of Hazzard), and me as a white belt.

I wasn't always dead sexy. For a while I was a teenager.

Getting my Brown Belt in Chinese Kenpo from Dave Kovar. Earlier on in my path and defiliety part of my vision quest.

Some time in high school, maybe my Junior year?

My junior year in college. I grew a ponytail for a while because I thought Interview with the Vampire was cool. Don't judge me.

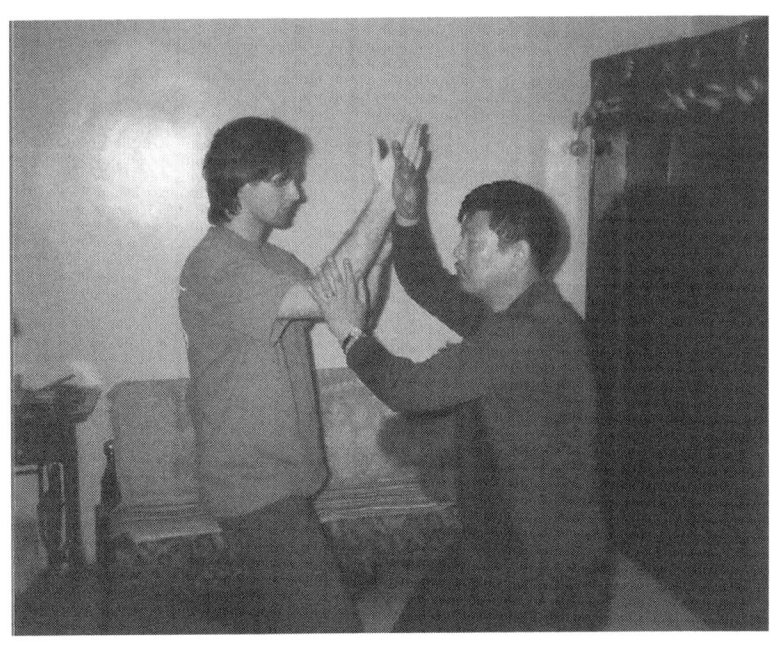

Training with Lui Chan Shan when I lived in China. Good times. Living in Northern China is a lot like a Seinfeld episode. You always take off your shoes and pants, leaving only your "leg sweater" on. It was pretty cold there.

Getting beaten on by George Xu. Story of my life.

Hanging out in China again. I didn't actually get to train with this giant sword, but I got to pose with it. So there's that. Probably for the best. We were on a super slick floor that my shoes wouldn't grip on. And do you know how hard it is to get a size 13 shoe in China?

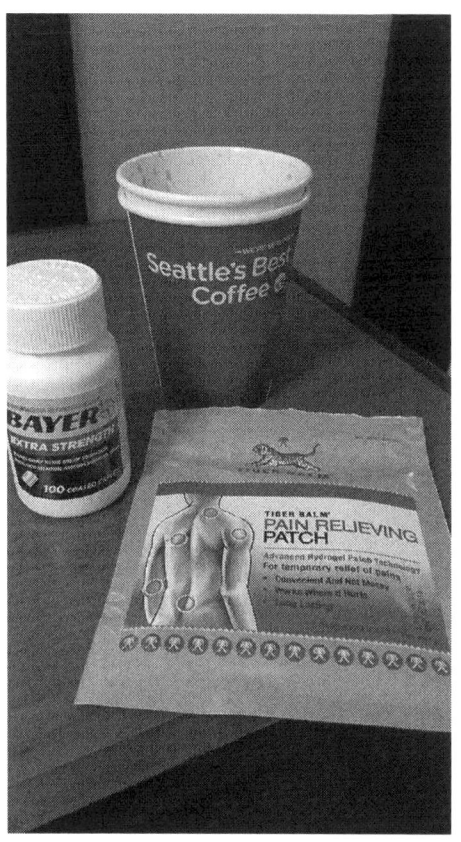

Ahh, breakfast after taking the Superfoot System Black Belt test. I flew down to Mobile, Alabama for that and then flew up to Boston for a Krav Maga Test the next day. It's hard to Krav Maga stuff when you can barely walk- but I made it work.

Krav Maga training just outside of Boston, MA. An awesome time and I'm ready for more!

Printed in Great Britain
by Amazon